Bill Lawry's
GREAT CRICKET
JOKE BOOK

BILL LAWRY with **JIM MAIN**

Published by
Information Australia
A.C.N. 006 042 173
75-77 Flinders Lane
Melbourne VIC 3000
Telephone: (03) 9654 2800
Fax: (03) 9650 5261

The National Library of Australia
Cataloguing-in-Publication entry:
Lawry, Bill.
Bill Lawry's great cricket joke book.

ISBN 1 86350 244 0

1. Cricket - Humor. 2. Australian wit and humor. I. Main, Jim, 1943- . II. Title.

796.3580207

Cover Design/Desktop: Paul Martinsen, Q Graphics
Cartoons: Andrew Fyfe

Printed and bound in Australia by Australian Print Group

About the Authors

Bill Lawry

Bill Lawry captained Australia from 1967-8 to 1970-1. He scored 18,734 first-class runs. He's been a star of the Channel Nine cricket team for two decades.

Jim Main

Jim Main was born to be a sports writer. He worked on the *Daily Express* in London before before winning a Walkley Award (Australian journalism's most prestigious award) in 1973 with the Melbourne *Herald*. Jim is the author of more than 30 books.

Andrew Fyfe

Andrew has featured as the on-air cartoonist for "Hey Hey It's Saturday" for the past fourteen years, in which his lightning fast sketches using "pen cam" have become an integral part of the show.

Andrew's work has also appeared in numerous publications over the years including *TV Week* and *Mad Magazine*.

Contents

It's All Happening

From the earliest years of cricket in Australia there have been what we love to describe as "characters", cricketers like Merv Hughes or Max Walker or, in the current era, Shane Warne. Cricketers who could get the crowd behind them and make them laugh.

Psychologists could suggest that this has been a fine thread through more than a century of Australian cricket because of the examples set by the very earliest Australian stars of the game, with the more extrovert personalities trying to live up to historical expectations.

For example, there can be little doubt that the most extrovert Australian cricket star of the nineteenth century was an Aborigine who revelled in the name of Dick-a-Dick and not only entertained crowds with his cricket prowess, but also threw boomerangs. It also could be suggested he was the prototype for AFL umpires as he also excelled in the difficult art of running backwards.

One of Dick-a-Dick's other tricks was to take a shield on to an oval and allow spectators to throw cricket balls at him, while he used the shield for protection. There were numerous reports of Dick-a-Dick fending off several balls at a time, but there is not one reference to anyone hitting him.

Then, when cricket became a much more serious game, Australia and England played Test matches. The first of these was played at the MCG in 1877 and, from the very start, there were what could only be described as "incidents".

For example, England's Thomas Armitage was so frustrated by the batting of Australia's Charles Bannerman that he resorted to bowling full tosses way above the batsman's head in the hope that the ball would miss Bannerman's head and bat to land on the bails. Fat chance!

Bannerman went on to make the first Test century - 165 (retired hurt after having a finger split by a delivery from George Ulyett) - and help give Australia a victory to embarrass the cocky tourists.

The colonial press had a field day and Marcus Clarke, in a pamphlet titled *The Future Australian Race*, wrote that the colonies were reaping the benefit of "the best bone and sinew of Cornwall, the best muscle of Yorkshire, the keenest brains of Cockneydom who had come to Bathurst, Ballarat and Bendigo, during the gold rushes".

Note the very British ingredients of this "super" Australian race. What would Clarke think of future Australian Test stars Len Pascoe (born of Yugoslav parents and whose surname originally was Durtanovich), Mike Veletta or Mike Kasprowicz or even New South Wales batsman Richard Chee Quee?

Fred Spofforth -
self-proclaimed "demon"

Then, in the Second Test, Australia produced the first of its long list of colorful fast bowlers. Fred Spofforth was not nicknamed The Demon for nothing, even though it now appears he bowled at little more than medium pace. At the time, however, he was thought to be the ultimate fast bowler, with a truly fiery temperament.

No-one knows for sure how Spofforth won his nickname, but there are suspicions he came up with the title himself. After all, one of his favorite post-match chants was "Ain't I a demon? Ain't I a demon?".

Spofforth, of course, played a huge part in the birth of the Ashes tradition. He was Australia's bowling hero in the famous victory over England at The Oval in 1882 and was carried shoulder-high off the ground by jubilant teammates. He took a total of 14 wickets (7/46 and 7/44) in Australia's first Test win in England.

It was after this England defeat that Reginald Brooks wrote an obituary for English cricket in the Sporting Times. It read:

"In affectionate remembrance of English Cricket, which died at The Oval on 29 August 1882. Deeply lamented by a large circle of sorrowing friends and acquaintances.

"R.I.P.

"NB: The body will be cremated and the ashes taken to Australia."

The Ashes legend was born, and over more than a century, there have been sensations and scandals, jubilation and jokes, cavaliers and clowns. Ashes series always have been serious business, but there always have been lighter moments, as this book illustrates only too well.

There even have been times when jokes have been perpetrated, only to fall flat because the competition was so vigorous, the concentration so intense. For example, there was the time Australia's Allan Border went to the crease and was confronted by England's Allan Lamb wearing a plastic duck's bill. Yet Border was so intent on doing his duty for his country that he still cannot recall this incident.

And, of course, this refers to all Test cricket as, indeed, competition between the cricketing nations has intensified over recent years. Whereas Sri Lanka once might have been considered "easy meat", it now is the one-day World Cup champion, and defeated England in a one-off Test in 1998.

Try telling the West Indies that only Ashes series are important, or try telling South Africa that it is not as competitive as Australia. More than one Test cricketer has admitted over the years that the game at this level can be anything but enjoyable. The pressure can be too intense for some cricketers.

Some, of course, thrive on this type of pressure and others relieve the pressure by taking a lighter approach, through banter and practical jokes. And there always have been times when laughter can be the best possible way to ease the sometimes heavy burden of representing your country.

I did this myself although, I must admit, my appointment as Australian captain made me take myself much more seriously. Captaincy means responsibility, although this does not necessarily mean I did not enjoy myself at all times as an Australian Test representative. There always was time for the lighter side of cricket, as this book well illustrates.

On a personal level, I always have had a dry sense of humor and, I would like to believe, this is reflected in my work as a commentator with the Nine network. After all, cricket telecasts without humor could bore viewers. Why do you think we have cracks and quips and, of course, the now famous banner competition? I even have been forced to laugh at myself when, for example, someone waves a huge sheet bearing the words "Bill Lawry's hanky".

Where did I get my sense of humor? To be honest, I don't really know and it must be something developed from a very early age. My father, a working class man (a tobacco stripper) enoyed life to the full, but I could never describe him as a humorist.

Rather, he was your average suburban dad who cared deeply for his family and his hobbies, which, in his case, were his pigeons and sport. He loved his cricket and his football (supporting the once-famous Fitzroy in the Victorian Football league).

I inherited Dad's love of pigeons and sport, and although I was never a good footballer, I also followed Fitzroy's fortunes. My first sports loves were cricket and baseball and, thankfully, they complemented each other. It therefore is interesting to reflect that several other Australian Test batsmen - Ian and Greg Chappell and Neil Harvey - also played baseball as youngsters.

I suppose my first taste of cricket humor was with the old radio broadcasts of Ashes matches played in England. Older readers would recall that there was no ball-by-ball description but, rather, a variety show with intermittent reports of wickets or batting milestones.

These broadcasts in Melbourne were on 3DB and the variety probably was as popular as the intermittent reports on what was happening in England. But, no matter what was being broadcast - a song, a comedy routine or whatever - the fall of a wicket meant an interruption.

I can recall that the fall of a wicket meant the introduction of "Ricketty Kate" and, when Australia was batting, I dreaded this interruption. But, with England batting, my ears strained in case I missed a wicket. Now, of course, there are direct telecasts and cricket fans know precisely what is happening at all times.

However, the Nine team has never forgotten that its primary duties are to inform AND entertain and that's why there always are light-hearted comments and a little fun in all our telecasts.

I started my first-class career with Victoria at a time when television was just starting in Australia so, in reality, my career has coincided with the telecasting of games.

Most Test and State cricketers these days tape their performances so that, in retirement, they can look back on what they achieved. Unfortunately, there was no television in Australia when I pulled on the navy blue cap of Victoria for the first time.

That was in the 1954-5 season (television arrived in Australia in 1956) when I was selected to play for a Victorian XI for a match against the Warracknabeal Cricket Association. Then, at the start of the next season, I made 183 for a Victorian Second XI against South Australia. If only I had a videotape of that innings...

My first Sheffield Shield match was against Western Australia at the Junction Oval (the MCG was being prepared for the Olympics) in February 1956. And I am glad there is no tape of this match as I made just three runs.

It was around this time that I got my nickname of "Phanto", coined by teammate Dick Maddocks, who saw me reading a *Phantom* comic. The name has stuck through the years and I still turn my head when someone calls out "Hey, Phanto".

There also was the nickname coined by English journalist Ian Wooldridge later in my career. After what he had thought was a painstaking innings, he dubbed me "the corpse with pads on", and I still get the occasional jibe about this.

But, I get ahead of myself. As a rookie first-class cricketer, I soon learned that it paid to be one of the boys and ready for a joke or two. Sure, we played cricket as if our lives depended on it, but there also were fun times, especially when we went interstate.

Fortunately, I got among the runs during the 1960-1 season and, to my great surprise, was selected for the tour of England that year. Would you believe that I was working as a plumber on a building site (the Royal Children's Hospital, Melbourne) when given the good news?

In those days, the tour took seven and a half months, including sailing time to and from England. Naturally, you get to know your teammates very, very well and, on my first international tour, I soon realised that Frank Misson and Graham McKenzie were what I referred to earlier as "great characters".

In particular, Misson was full of life and good humor. A fair-haired fellow with a wicked smile, Misson always was playing one practical joke or another on that tour and one is related later in this book.

Misson played in just two Tests on that 1961 tour of England and perhaps was a little unlucky not to have established himself as a permanent member of the Australian side. Overall, he played just five Tests, but I'll never forget the wonderful camaraderie he helped create in England in 1961.

I must admit I was involved in a number of practical jokes with Misson, although I now am not sure about who was responsible for the trick of splashing "ink" down the front of shirts.

The trick was to pretend to stagger, a bottle of "ink" in hand. The "ink", a lurid green, would splash all over the victim's shirt and there always was a hell of a kerfuffle as there was such a mess.

But within 10 minutes or so the stain would disappear. The liquid used in these pranks was invisible ink bought at a trick shop.

McKenzie was just 20 years of age when he went on that tour and, thank goodness he was there. Apart from his great sense of humor, McKenzie played a pivotal role in retaining the Ashes.

The Fourth Test, at Old Trafford, was a thriller. We made just 190 in the first innings, with England then scoring 367. With each Australian wicket that fell in the second innings, our situation looked grimmer and grimmer.

I managed to score a century (102) but, by the time the ninth wicket fell, we still led by a mere 157 runs - hardly enough against a strong England batting line-up. However, we had not counted on the determination of Alan Davidson and young McKenzie, who teamed up for a remarkable tenth wicket partnership.

Davidson was at his determined best when McKenzie strode purposefully to the crease and, by the time the 98-run partnership was broken, McKenzie had made 32 and Davidson was 77 not out. Australia eventually set England a target of 256 for victory - getable but tricky.

Thankfully, England captain Ted Dexter was an adventurous soul and his team chased victory, rather than settle for a draw. However, England was 1/150 before Aussie skipper Richie Benaud got among the wickets. We won by 54 runs, with Benaud taking 6/70.

One of my images from that match is of Davidson slumped in a corner after his courageous last-wicket partnership with McKenzie and telling Benaud: "Now let's get stuck into them. We can do these jokers, Rich."

It was during this trip that we were introduced to the Duke of Edinburgh, with Australian 'keeper Wally Grout coming up with one of the best lines of all time. In fact, it was so good that Grout often used to tell the tale and teammate Ken Mackay even wrote about it in his book *Slasher Opens Up*.

Grout was sporting a black eye and, as the Duke stopped to have a word with him, could not help but wince at the thought of having a shiner the color of charcoal and the size of an egg.

The Duke advised Grout: "I suggest you put some steak on that eye."

To which Grout replied: "We eat all our steak, sir."

In many ways Grout typified the grizzled Australian cricket veteran and I count myself fortunate to have been one of his teammates. He was a fabulous 'keeper and, in fact, Australia has been blessed with the quality of its men behind the stumps.

We currently have one of the best the game has seen in Ian Healy and, of course, there have been such great champions as

Jack Blackham, known as "the prince of wicketkeepers", Sammy Carter (an undertaker), Barry Jarman, Gil Langley, Rodney Marsh, Bert Oldfield, Brian Taber and Don Tallon - among others.

I played a lot of my Test cricket in the same side as Jarman, who had the distinction of captaining Australia in the Fourth Test against England in 1968 when I had to pull out of the side with a broken finger.

Jarman played just 19 Tests, but this figure could have been much greater if he had not been understudy to the great Wally Grout for so long and there were many cricket judges who believed Jarman was the second best 'keeper in the world (behind Grout) at that time.

But at least Jarman played Test cricket and captained Australia. Another fine Australian wicketkeeper of my era did not play a single Test, yet twice toured with the Australian team - to India and to South Africa.

Of course, I am referring to my former Victorian teammate Ray "Slug" Jordon, surely one of the greatest characters of the game and still regarded as one of sport's leading identities in his home town of Melbourne.

Also a fine footballer (he played in the Victorian Football Association with the Coburg club), Jordon had a horror start to his first-class cricket career and men of lesser character would have called it quits.

Not Raymond Clarence Jordon, who not only conceded 12 byes from the first three balls he faced as Victorian 'keeper, (see later in this book), but also dropped several chances. From that inauspicious debut, Jordon grew in stature as a 'keeper and as one of the bubbliest personalities in cricket.

The only way you could shut him up was to put a gag over his mouth. He was always chirping one comment or another and probably was one of the game's first great sledgers. He had a comment for every rival batsman and, at times, his language was colorful - to say the least.

There are several Slug Jordon yarns in this book but, for good measure, let me tell you of when "wrong-footed" Victorian pace man Alan "Froggy" Thomson was selected for Australia during the 1970-1 tour by England.

There was considerable criticism of Thomson's selection north of the Murray and questions were asked about the wisdom of playing a bowler with such an unusual technique. Jordon told Thomson not to worry about the criticism and added: "Anyway, the way you're bowling, everyone else has been bowling the wrong way."

Jordon fully supported his teammate, which, in one way was unusual. You see, Thomson was a senior Victorian Football League umpire and Jordon has spent most of his life cursing football umpires.

Another great character early in my Test career was Johnny Martin, a country boy who was universally liked and even carried the tag "the little favorite". Originally from the tiny country town of Burrell Creek, New South Wales, Martin lived up to the saying that you could take the boy out of the country, but couldn't take the country out of the boy.

Martin, a fine spinner and more-than-useful batsman, was a wonderful tourist as he kept everyone happy and could produce a party out of thin air, just as he did in Salisbury during the 1966-7 tour of South Africa.

We were having a very quiet night when some of the boys decided that it would be good to have a party. The only problem was that we didn't known anyone in this neck of the woods and would have to party by ourselves. Martin solved this problem by telephoning the local police and inviting them to join us for a few drinks. We had a great time.

Martin also was a noted big-hitter and his big ambition was to smash a six at every ground he played. I don't know whether or not he achieved this ambition, but I would like to think he did as he died of heart problems in 1992, just short of his 61st birthday. He deserved a much longer innings.

Then, of course, there were characters like Doug Walters, the boy from Dungog. Walters hit the headlines in a big way when he hit centuries in his first two Tests to become an instant national hero.

Walters also hit the headlines for his attempt to set beer-drinking records on flights around the world. I am not sure who now holds the record for drinking on flights between Australia and England, but I believe it is either Walters or his good mate Rodney Marsh and, I further believe, this record stands at something like 40 cans of beer.

Legend has it that after one beery flight to England Marsh even had a nightcap at his hotel before catching a long, long sleep.

Walters somehow defied all the logic that sportsmen should keep themselves fit. Off-field he was always dragging on a cigarette, loved his beer and spent most of his time in the dressing rooms playing cards.

In his book *One For The Road*, he even tells of the time in South Africa in 1970 that he had a heavy night and woke to a knock on the door. It was a waiter holding a tray of six bottles of beer. Room-mate Brian Taber had made the order in the wee hours of the morning and the pair of them decided to have a hair of the dog.

The problem was that the Australian tourists were scheduled to play a local side and, as captain, I told Walters he was to bat at number three instead of his usual fourth-wicket down. This meant he would have little rest, unless Keith Stackpole and I had a big opening partnership.

Walters, in his book, takes up the tale: "I'd just scrambled into my creams and donned the pads when a roar from the crowd told me just what I didn't want to know; someone was out (Stackpole), and the innings was only five minutes old...

"So there I am, standing out in the middle of the Newlands Grounds in Cape Town trying to find Mike Procter. I know he's somewhere down there by the sightscreen at the other end, but I can't quite make him out. And I'm wondering how clearly I'm going to see him when he unleashes the first thunderbolt and if I'm going to see the first ball at all."

As Walters points out in his book, he need not have worried. He not only survived the initial Procter onslaught, but went on to score a century - his only "ton" of the tour.

It was during this tour that I knew with absolute certainty that my days as a prankster on the team were over. I was older and, much more importantly, the Australian captain. As I wrote earlier, it just was not possible to play jokes on the boys and then crack the whip.

Sure, I still had fun but captaincy involves much more diplomacy and maturity and, of course, considerable restraint. I had other matters on my mind, especially as, in hindsight, the 1970 tour of South Africa was the beginning of the end of my captaincy of Australia as the Springboks - as they then were known (now the Proteas) - absolutely caned us.

Then, against England in Australia, Ray Illingworth's team took a 1-0 lead going into the final Test of the series, and I got the chop. I heard the news on the radio but, contrary to popular opinion, this did not worry me.

This was normal practice at that time, although I believe Ian Chappell, the man who replaced me as skipper, once remarked: "It won't happen to me." Thankfully, cricketers now get the news - good or bad - before the media gets it.

I did not know it at the time, but my Test career was over. I not only was dumped as captain, but lost my place as an opening batsman and was never able to regain it. England won that final Test by 62 runs to take the series 2-0 and, a few years later, I retired from first-class cricket.

At 38 years of age and, having played cricket at first-class level for almost two decades, I wondered if I had a future in the game. Sure, I could have coached but, in hindsight, I was destined to take up commentary work.

It all started when I did some work with my old mate Doug Ring on Seven's popular Sunday show *World of Sport*. From there, I called the increasingly popular one-day games with Ring and Mike Williamson on Seven and also did a bit of work with Channel 0 (now 10) as its cricket commentator.

But how was I to know then that my commentary work would take off in a way I could hardly have expected when I nervously spoke my first words into a microphone? And, of course, I owe everything to the Nine network and the birth of World Series Cricket in 1977 for my longevity in cricket broadcasting.

When WSC started in extremely controversial circumstances following the great cricket schism, I took a telephone call from PBL Sports Pty Ltd's Austin Robertson, asking me whether I would like to join the Nine team for these telecasts.

Strangely enough, I was not all that interested at first. A traditionalist at heart, I was worried about the future of the game and what WSC would do to the traditions of cricket. Finally, however, I was convinced to join Nine when invited by my first Test captain, Richie Benaud, whom I regard as the doyen of cricket commentators.

To be invited by Benaud to join the team was an extreme honor and I could hardly refuse. Besides, Benaud convinced me that cricket would be better off for the introduction of World Series Cricket. He was most persuasive.

I enjoyed my work on these WSC matches more than I ever could have imagined and, two years later, Channel 9 won the right to telecast the official Australian Cricket Board matches, enabling me to continue my broadcasting career.

I have worked with many wonderful commentators over the past 20 years, with Benaud at the top of the tree. Others include Greg and Ian Chappell, Michael Holding, Geoff Boycott, Tony Greig, Max Walker, David Gower, Doug Walters, Simon O'Donnell and Tony Cosier.

Their company has been most enjoyable, even if there have been one or two mishaps. For example, I could have turned the air "blue" if I had been at the microphone when I tripped over a crate of milk. Fortunately, it was just before we were about to go on air.

Then there was the time Benaud was hit on the head by a prop, just as he was welcoming viewers to the Gabba. But, being the ultimate professional, he did not miss a beat and did not complain - until he was off-camera.

A lot of people ask me what it is like to be a cricket commentator and, I must admit, I tell them it is the best job in the world. How could it be better for someone who loves the game so much?

However, I must admit, it is so professional these days that there is little time for socialising or even for a bit of banter. We fly all around Australia every summer and hardly a day goes by when there is not some work to be done, even if not all of it is on-camera.

For example, cricketers get rests between the one-day internationals. Australia might play England one day and Sri Lanka will take on England the next day. This means the Australians get a rest day. But not the commentators! We are at EVERY match and, believe it or not, it can be tiring, especially when you consider how much flying is involved.

The only time we really get to relax is of an evening and even then we sometimes are a bit bushed. Although the cricket public has this perception that Tony Greig and I are sworn enemies, nothing could be further from the truth, and I often find myself relaxing with him over dinner after a long day in the commentary box.

We are very good mates and any antagonism is a mirage and stems only from the fact that we might have different opinions on certain aspects of cricket or, perhaps, on the tactics and/or progress of a match.

Tony also is extremely professional in everything he does and, by the way, covers far more cricket than I do. For example, Tony might go to South Africa or the sub-continent, while I go overseas only for Ashes tours of England. Tony also went to Malaysia in 1998 for the Kuala Lumpur Commonwealth Games, while I watched all the action from the comfort of my lounge room.

I prefer it that way as I am not a great traveller, unless it is to the United Kingdom. I just love being in England and jump at every opportunity to go there - for several reasons.

JUST TESTING PLAYERS COMFORT LEVEL!

Firstly, any Ashes series is exciting and I would not want to miss them for quids, whether they be in Australia or in England. And, of course, the Tests in England bring back many memories of when I was playing at such famous venues as Old Trafford, The Oval, Lord's, Edgbaston and Trent Bridge.

Also, I have a great number of English friends, especially from the pigeon-fanciers' fraternity, all over the UK. I often stay with these friends and, when they come to Australia, they stay with me and wife Joy.

I love these social occasions and, added to the pleasure of visiting these friends in England, is the fact that I just love the English countryside, with its rolling green hills and gentle scenery.

Imagine the setting! A beautifully manicured English wicket, a pale blue sky, a warm sun and a light breeze. This is typical of cricket in England, even though many Australians have images of drizzling rain at Manchester or Leeds.

It is my idea of heaven, especially as I can meet my friends after a day's play and talk about pigeons. I know this might not be everyone's cup of tea, but I just love it and I always count the days to Ashes series in England.

In Australia, the Channel Nine team criss-crosses the country and, by the end of the summer, we have had just about enough.... until next time. And, when spring is in the air, there is an extra bounce to William Morris Lawry's step.

As for today's cricketers, it has been suggested that we no longer have characters in the game. To a certain extent this might be true, as there does not appear to be a Merv Hughes or a Max Walker on the scene.

I can understand the cricket public's thinking on this, but it must be realised that cricket now is much more professional than it was even six or seven years ago. Test cricketers now earn very good money and must have a totally professional approach.

I therefore doubt if we'll see too many extrovert and wildly chariasmatic cricketers emerge in the modern era. Champion leg-spinner Shane Warne probably is the closest we'll get these days to the image of the flamboyant cricketer.

He might wear ear-rings and celebrate victories with wild jigs that annoy the hell out of his English critics, but he takes his cricket very, very seriously because it is his livelihood. And a very good one at that.

I therefore can assure you that the current crop of first-class cricketers still have a ball and still play practical jokes. The evidence of this is in some the yarns they spin later in this book.

Also, there are your yarns, of country cricket cock-ups and suburban slogs. Then there are the funny, unusual, bizarre and even tragic incidents from more than 100 years of cricket. And, finally, there are humorous, ironic and poignant quotes from those who have been involved in the greatest game of all.

Read and enjoy!

Phantom tales

After a life-time in cricket, I have seen many funny incidents and been involved in many pranks. Here, for your enjoyment, is just a sample.

Once bitten...

One of the great characters in my early years as a Victorian State cricketer was John "Strawberry" Power, a superb fast bowler who had a magnificent action and a tremendous outswinger. Power twice took three wickets in an over against powerful NSW batting line-ups, so certainly was no slouch with the ball.

Power was, to put in bluntly, a bit of a larrikin. Although totally dedicated to his cricket, he was always good for a laugh. In fact, he could have been the prototype for Max Walker.

For example, there was the time he was playing for Victoria in a Sheffield Shield match against South Australia at the MCG when my Northcote teammate John Wildsmith made his debut for the State. Wildsmith, a very good spinner, was understandably nervous and did not quite know what to expect when he took the field on the first day.

Power, as usual, opened the bowling, but when he asked umpire Bill Smythe for a marker for his run-up, Smythe told him he had forgotten to put one in his pocket. "Don't worry, China (his nickname for everyone he met)," Power shrugged. "I'll make do."

Then, at the end of his first over, Power asked Wildsmith to retrieve the "marker". Knowing what the umpire had told Power, the newcomer was understandably puzzled. But, wanting to make a good impression on his debut, did as he was told.

He walked over to where Power had started his run, and discovered a pair of false teeth nestling on the hallowed MCG turf.

It was just one example of Power's unorthodox cricketing nature and, in a District match against Prahran, he managed to upset one of the game's greatest identities - Prahran skipper and former Test all-rounder Sam Loxton.

Power's offence? He took a superb catch at mid-on. The only trouble was that he deliberately caught the ball with his cap, from a return catch from the outfield, but Power was prepared to concede the five runs for this offence by having a little light-hearted relief from the pressure of a tight match.

Also, I'll never forget when he played his last match for Victoria. He was given the honor of leading the field onto the ground - and he was wearing the bright blue with seagull motif cap of the Surfers' Paradise club.

Beau Brummel is nailed

Former Australian Test captain Richie Benaud was ahead of his time in almost everything he did. He not only was a daring and innovative captain, but also created cricket history by being the first practising journalist to captain Australia. And he almost certainly was way ahead of the rest of the cricket field in terms of fashion. He was a real Beau Brummel.

Anyone who saw Benaud play cricket would remember that his whites were whiter than white and his shirt collar raised to set a trend for the era. He did not have a single hair out of place.

Off the field, he was even more immaculate. If there was a new style of suit from Italy, Benaud would be wearing it. If there was

Richie Benaud - shoes nailed to a floor

a new style in ties, Benaud would have a dozen of them. He also was the slowest dresser in the Australian team as he always took infinite care in his appearance.

In fact, it became a standing joke on Australian tours that after a day's play there always would be 16 cricketers on a bus waiting for Benaud. He then would appear as if going to a cocktail party.

This became a bit too much for NSW pace bowler Frank Misson, who was a bit of a Merv Hughes character but a bit more subtle. Frank got a few of us together with an idea he had come up with to teach Benaud to be a tad quicker in the dressing room.

Benaud, at that time, had a pair of slip-on shoes that were the pride of his wardrobe. Slip-ons were radically new in an era in which lace-up shoes were almost a uniform in the western world.

Benaud had only just bought his slip-ons and they were always polished to a mirror.

After one day's play we all decided to stay in the rooms while Benaud dressed. We watched as he carefully put on his fine cotton shirt and then his sharply-creased trousers. He watched as he was infinitely careful in knotting his tie and, finally, he got to the slip-on shoes - carefully placed in front of his locker.

Benaud slipped ever so comfortably into them but, when he tried to walk, he almost fell on his face. The shoes had been nailed to the floor. I still do not know who nailed the shoes, but I suspect the man who gave us the idea in the first place - Misson.

Besides, as Benaud stumbled, he screamed: "I'll kill you, Misson." Frank, therefore, was good enough to take the blame, which certainly was an act of courage considering how Benaud was so careful with his appearance.

Which brings me to one of cricket's long-held rumors that Laurie Nash was banished from Test cricket in the 1930s after having nailed the great Don Bradman's boots to the MCG dressing-room floor.

Nash, who played just two Tests, certainly was a great cricket talent who probably deserved greater recognition and it seems he did upset authorities during his brief Test career as a pace bowler.

From what I have heard - and it might well be an apocryphal tale - Nash was banished from the Test scene for appearing shoeless and sockless on the MCG members' balcony and dangling his feet over a rail.

Nash certainly was a character and, possibly one of Australia's greatest all-round sports stars. Of course, he achieved fame as a champion footballer with South Melbourne in the '30s and once kicked 18 goals for Victoria in a match against South Australia - after being switched from defence in the second quarter.

One of Nash's most endearing charms was his own belief in the enormity of his sports prowess. Whenever was asked to nominate the greatest footballer of all time, he would reply: "I look at him in the mirror every morning when I shave."

Knifing the manager

The manager of the Australian team to England in 1961 was Syd Webb QC, who not only was an Australian Cricket Board of Control director, but also the board's legal adviser and one of the greatest socialisers of his era.

Webb, who was as wide as he was tall, loved cocktail parties and making speeches. Very early on the tour we got to learn his favorite message by heart. It would be: "I am off to a very important meeting." He then would tuck his satchel under his arm and march off to have a couple of whiskies with a County club secretary.

Webb, however, was at his best when introducing team members to royalty. Barely 160cm tall, Webb would stretch himself, blissfully unaware that by thrusting his head skywards to appear taller, his pants shot up several centimetres and his socks would show well above his shoes.

He was a wonderful character who not only was the butt of many pranks, but always took them in the very best of spirits. For example, my good Australian teammate Frank Misson always would wait until we all were seated at a function before he would ask a waitress to page Mr Webb. I think dear old Webby fell for this joke at almost every function, and always took it gracefully.

And, heaven knows, few men of his standing would have forgiven us for what we did to him at a Clarence House cocktail party hosted by the Queen Mother when we came up with the idea of making him appear to be a kleptomaniac.

Misson followed him around Clarence House and, every now and then, would slip a knife or a spoon into his jacket pocket. I still don't how we got away with it as Webb clanged with every step he took.

Then, when it was time to leave, assistant manager Ray Steele mentioned to one of the Queen Mother's household that Webb had a "slight problem" and that he should be asked to empty his pockets in private.

I can still hear Webb scream "bloody Lawry" as he put his hands in his pockets to discover the knives and spoons planted there by

Misson. But I had such a good laugh I was more than happy to take the blame.

Then there was the time that we decided to have a bit of fun with Webb's ubiquitous satchel, which was always at hand. In fact, we often thought Webb went to bed with the satchel by his side.

Every time he had one of his "important meetings" his right hand would shoot out for his satchel. We therefore decided during one County match that we would tie a string around the handles and have the strings stretched over a ceiling beam.

Webb, as was his habit just before the tea break, announced that he had to attend "an important meeting", that is, have a whisky or two. He reached out for his satchel and, as he grabbed it, two team members yanked on the string and pulled him and the bag towards the ceiling. We left him there for several minutes and I am sure that he was in real dread that he would miss the best part of his "special meeting".

One of the other tricks we played on the unfortunate Webb was through the use of a rubber device similar to a whoopy-cushion. But, instead of embarrassing Webby with strange and inexplicable noises appearing to come from his nether regions, we used to place our special device under the table cloth and under his plate at meals.

Every time Webb would try to put knife and fork to food, the plate would wobble, courtesy of a puff of air through a tube. And, of course, at the end of that tube was either Misson or myself. I don't think dear old Webby ever woke up to this trick and he must have thought that English dining tables were very insecure indeed.

Well and truly caught

For reasons unknown, I have become a central figure in a yarn about England fast bowler Fred Trueman and butter-fingered fielder David Sheppard. I have no recollection of the incident and I am certain I was not involved, but the tale has been told so often that there must be an element of truth in it with, I believe, another batsman - I am almost certain it was Peter Burge - involved.

It seems that on a tour of Australia in the '60s, the unfortunate Sheppard dropped an easy chance at backward square leg during one of the first matches of the tour. Then, in the next match in Adelaide, South Australian batsman Les Favell, who really could thrash a ball, hooked straight to backward square leg early in his innings. Sheppard easily got under the ball, and dropped it.

If looks could have killed, they would have buried Sheppard the next day, especially as Favell went on to make a big score. Then, in Sydney on the next tour match, Trueman dropped one short to Neil Harvey, who hooked into the air.

"I won't miss this one," Sheppard told himself as he raced to get under the ball. And down it sailed, comfortably into his hands - only to bobble out at the last second. And Harvey went on to make a double century.

The England selectors met the next week to name their side for the First Test in Brisbane and, when skipper Ted Dexter announced the 11, Trueman put up his hand and asked if he could make a point.

Dexter nodded his agreement, so Trueman said: "David's dropped so many chances that I believe his inclusion in the team could be costly."

To which Dexter explained: "We've already discussed the matter and we have decided that we need David's batting. Anyway, he'll be fielding at fine leg and third man, well away from chances."

When Australia batted first on a greenish wicket, Trueman was in his element. He whistled down short deliveries to unnerve the batsmen and Australia soon found itself two for next to nothing.

The next man in was the scourge of the England bowlers, the big-hitting Peter Burge. It therefore was imperative that England get his wicket early to prevent an Australian fightback. Trueman therefore had fire steaming from his nostrils.

He tore down the wicket, dropped the ball short and Burge hooked. The ball flew high and wide, and Sheppard raced almost 100 metres as Trueman watched gape-jawed in the almost certain knowledge that his teammate either would not get to the ball in time or that, even if he did, the chance would go through his butter fingers.

Sheppard finally dived, threw his right hand high into the air - and the ball stuck. It was a sensational catch, one of the best ever taken in Test cricket. Sheppard was so jubilant he danced in the deep, throwing the ball high into the air no less than five times.

Finally, he heard Trueman bellowing from the wicket area: "Hey, David, throw the ball back. It was a no-ball and they've already taken three runs."

Well, that's my story, anyway!

And, talking of butter-fingered fielders, England's Keith Fletcher had a terrible reputation for putting down chances and one of Trueman's favorite stories concerns the time vandals dug up the pitch overnight during the England-Australia Third Test at Headingley in 1975.

The way Trueman tells it, the culprits - highlighting the plight of convicted armed robber George Davis - were sent to jail and asked the former England fast bowler to visit them so they could make a request.

Intrigued, Trueman made the visit and was asked whether he would plead on their behalf.

"But you haven't been sentenced," Trueman says in telling the tale.

"Yeah, but we've been led to believe that for ruining a Test match we are going to be thrown from a cricket pavilion roof...with Keith Fletcher catching us."

Howzat, Don?

Victorian wicketkeeper Ray Jordon was unlucky not to have worn the baggy green cap of Australia as a Test cricketer. Jordon was a superb glove-man and a handy batsman, but always had either South Australia's Barry Jarman or New South Wales' Brian Taber just ahead of him.

Jordon was a superb all-rounder who was a wonderfully talented rover in the Victorian Football Association with the Coburg club. Later, he became one of the finest under-age football coaches in the game. And, throughout his sports career, he was a loveable larrikin. Loveable, that is, as long as he was on your side.

As a football coach, he could be very demanding as future Brownlow Medallist Jim Stynes discovered soon after arriving from Ireland to play the Australian code virtually sight unseen.

Stynes started with the Melbourne Under 19s, with Jordon as coach. On debut, Stynes fluffed what should have been a gimme goal and Jordon, unimpressed with his 18-year-old Irish recruit, bellowed for all to hear: "Take that big # ^ @*%! leprechaun off the ground."

TAKE THAT BIG
LEPRECHAUN
OFF THE GROUND!

"Slug" Jordon, who earned his nickname when accidentally shot during national service, was one of the first of cricket's notorious sledgers. In fact, he made life hell for batsmen and seemed to have individual comments for them all.

Yet Jordon's first-class cricket career started disastrously, simply because he under-estimated the speed of Victorian pace bowler Ian Meckiff, who was regarded as the fastest bowler in world cricket in the mid-60s.

Jordon had kept wickets exceptionally well for the Carlton club in Melbourne District cricket, but obviously had never kept to a bowler anywhere near as fast as Meckiff and therefore greatly miscalculated when he marked out his usual 20 paces to stand behind the stumps on debut for Victoria.

Meckiff tore down the field and, whizz, the ball flew high over Jordon's head for four byes. Wow, Jordon must have thought! That really was fast. Meckiff tore in for his second delivery and, whizz, the ball again flew over Jordon's head to the boundary for four more byes.

Undeterred, Jordon steeled himself for the third delivery. Meckiff tore in, let the ball fly and, whizz, it again flew over Jordon's head to the boundary for four more byes. What a disastrous start to a first-class wicketkeeping career - three deliveries and the opposition had scored 0/12 - all from byes!

Jordon then stepped back a few paces to take Meckiff's deliveries at a comfortable waist-height and went on to become a reliable and often brilliant 'keeper who sometimes revelled in extraordinary performances.

For example, in a Sheffield Shield match against South Australia at the Adelaide Oval, Jordon stood up to the quickish bowling of Alan Connolly - no mean feat in itself - to stump Ian Chappell down the leg-side.

I know Ian Healy has made leg-side stumpings from the bowling of Shane Warne, but to do it from pace bowling is right out of the ordinary. But, to prove it was no fluke, Jordon then stumped Greg Chappell down the leg-side from another Connolly delivery.

Jordon was so pleased with his twin stumping efforts that he held the ball high in the air for all to see and I had no doubt he was making a point to the man in direct line of vision - Australian chairman of selectors Sir Donald Bradman.

Jordon, in hindsight, might have regretted this piece of showmanship. Who knows whether it ever cost him an Australian Test cap? Come to think of it, though, I doubt if Jordon would regret anything he ever did as he always has accepted life's challenges and setbacks and made the most of them.

Cooped up

Ray Jordon was one of the jokers in the Victorian pack and always good for a laugh. In fact, he always has had one of the most distinctive laughs I have ever heard, one you can hear him from miles. And he certainly had a good laugh at my expense early in my time as Victorian captain.

Soon after being appointed State cricket captain, a tremendous honor, I felt weighed down by responsibility. After all, I was just a young bloke who had been raised in the working class Melbourne suburb of Northcote, educated at Preston Technical School and trained as a plumber.

I felt very humble about the captaincy, especially as I was following in the footsteps of such great men as Bill Woodfull, Jack Ryder, Lindsay Hassett and Ian Johnson - all great Victorian captains.

I therefore decided that it would be a great idea to create team harmony by inviting the Victorian squad to my home at Reservoir for a barbeque, little knowing Jordon's reputation as a practical joker.

Halfway through the night, Jordon ambled up to me and asked me if it was true that I was a pigeon fancier.

"Yes," I replied proudly. "My pigeons are my pride and joy."

"Well, where are they?" Jordon asked. "I'd like to have a look at them."

I proudly puffed out my chest like a pigeon, so to speak, and told Jordon to follow me down the garden.

"There," I said, pointing to the loft. "That's where I keep them."

"Oh, but can I have a closer look?" Jordon asked.

"Sure," I replied and opened the loft door. And, no sooner had I stepped inside than Jordon shut the door and locked it.

"Now we can really enjoy ourselves," he laughed.

Mind your *#@^%$! language

England fast bowler Fred Trueman was one of the greatest characters to play cricket. A ferocious competitor, he had the killer instinct when he had a ball in his right hand. Off the field, he was great company and full of laughs.

Trueman, a truly great after dinner speaker, probably has spun

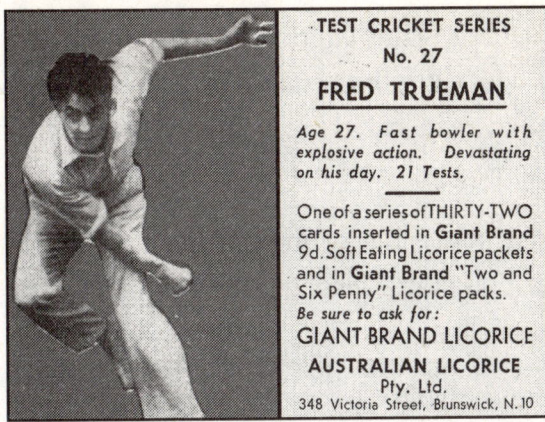

Fred Trueman - colorful language

more yarns than any other cricketer. Yet there is at least an element of truth in all his yarns and, for example, he loves telling the story of the time an English County match was played in a howling gale.

The batsmen and the fielders had trouble adjusting to the ferocity of the wind and the bails often were blown to the ground. Then, when the bails fluttered to the ground after one particular delivery, the batsman turned to the umpire and said: "The wind's done it again."

The umpire, however, had been around far too long for that trick and immediately turned to the batsman and said: "Yeah, the wind is strong, but I saw your foot hit the stumps and you're out."

This, by the way, is a Trueman yarn without a single expletive, with the big Yorkshireman famous for the color of his language. Yet, strangely enough, Trueman could get away with his particular brand of down-to-earth language.

For example, I recall the time I was sitting with Trueman and other cricketers during a match at the WACA late in my Test career. It was a hot, sunny afternoon and Trueman entertained all and sundry with his full repertoire of yarns, complete with numerous expletives. In fact, there were more four-letter words than you would come across at a bullocky's picnic.

The air was thick with swearing and cussing, but nobody seemed to mind, least of all the small group of little old ladies sitting in front of us.

Finally, one of the cricketers sitting with Trueman dropped a mildly offensive word. If my memory serves me correctly, he suggested there was an element of "bull...." in one of Trueman's colorful stories.

No sooner had the offensive word left his lips that one of the women turned around with the stern admonishment: "Would you please mind your language!"

This is a real-life Trueman story, as opposed to many that he has told over the years. For example, Trueman, enormously proud of being a Yorkshireman, often has told the slightly ribald tale of the two Yorkshiremen who went to see their County in action against bitter "War of the Roses" enemy Lancashire.

The two men settled in for the start of play, only for one of them to realise that he had left the picnic lunch at home. "I'm not going home to get it as Len Hutton is batting," he insisted.

His mate argued that he also wanted to see Hutton bat, but finally agreed to get the lunch and, on his return, said: "I've got bad news for you. I caught your wife in bed with your next door neighbor."

"Oh, I've got worse news for you," was the reply. "Hutton is out."

A case of mistaken identity

Remember the crack by England all-rounder Ian Botham about touring Pakistan? You know, the one about Pakistan being a good place to send your mother-in-law on an all expenses holiday?

Well, we thought the same about India when we toured there in 1969. But, of course, the India of 20 years ago was vastly different to what it is today and cricketers visiting the sub-continent now stay in luxurious hotels and even have specially prepared meals.

It was all so different in the '60s and Fred Trueman once re-marked that if you go for a swim in India you can be bitten by a water snake and die within seconds. Even worse, Trueman sug-gested, after three weeks of Indian food you go looking for a snake.

If the heat - or the snakes - did not get you, there was the almost ever-present diarrhoea. You had to be very, very careful with what you drank and even had to brush your teeth with bottled water.

The 1969 tour was quite an ordeal and I therefore could have done without one disturbance very early in the morning - after a night of tossing and turning in the heat - when awakened by angry knocks on my hotel room door.

I rubbed my eyes, padded across the room and opened the door to see Australian teammate Graham McKenzie waving a newspaper at me. "What do they mean by this?" he demanded. I had absolutely no idea why he was pushing the paper into my face, and told him so.

"Someone's got the wrong end of the stick," he fumed. "Just have a look."

My patience worn thin, I invited him into my room so I could read the paper. I groaned when I read the headline "Australians Told To Apologise Or Else", but then had to laugh when I read that McKenzie, aided by Ian Redpath, supposedly had been involved in an incident in which an Indian journalist had been thrown out of a room.

McKenzie might have been a fast bowler who could work up a fair head of steam against opposition batsmen, but he just was not the type to be involved in this type of incident and I could understand his anger and frustration.

But, the more I thought of McKenzie and the mild-mannered Redpath being involved in such an incident, the more I laughed. And the more I laughed, the more aggressive became Mckenzie's demands.

"Well," he insisted again. "What are you going to do about it?"

"I guess I'll have to meet with (tour manager) Fred Bennett and send the pair of you home."

McKenzie's face dropped a mile, until he saw me smile at his predicament. He finally knew that I knew it was a case of mistaken identity, especially as he and Redpath had an alibi for the time the reporter was supposed to have been thrown out of a room for asking offensive questions.

I always wondered what would have happened if Eric Freeman had been named in the report.

Tossed by the rain

I once had the eerie experience of playing in a Test match in which not a single ball was bowled. Yet it remains in the record books as an official Test simply because the respective captains, England's Ray Illingworth and I, tossed the coin.

Illingworth won the toss for the Test, at Melbourne late in 1970, and, with dark clouds scudding over the MCG, sent Australia in to bat. I returned to the dressing room where Keith Stackpole and I put on the pads.

We waited and we waited and we waited. The ran pelted down throughout the first day and, just as we seemed set to make a start on the second day, down it came again. In fact, Stacky and I must be the only two batsmen to wear the pads for the entire duration of a Test match.

It was, to say the least, an unnerving experience and, in the end, I would have given anything to get away from the claustrophobic atmosphere of the dressing room. By the time the Test was officially abandoned, on the fifth day, I was a mental wreck.

I recall that one Australian team group spent most of the waiting time playing cards. Other reads newspapers and magazines and others simply stretched out and snoozed. It was the ultimate proof that every cricketer behaves differently in dressing room situations.

For example, Doug Walters was the most relaxed character you would ever wish to see. Nothing seemed to faze him and, in fact, he had a trademark habit of leaving a lit cigarette in an ashtray and commenting: "Leave it there; I might be back soon."

His entire family must have had nerves of steel as I can recall the time his mother telephoned Lord's to give him a message. When told that her son had just gone out to bat, his mother replied: "Don't worry. I'll hang on."

England's Colin Cowdrey also was a cool customer and was nicknamed "Kipper" because of his habit of going to sleep as the incoming batsman.

In contrast, Australia's Norm O'Neill was a nervous wreck every time he put on his pads. He always wore yellow undersocks and I once saw him retch before an innings. But, once his feet hit the turf, all his nerves were banished and he deserved his reputation as one of the great attacking batsmen of world cricket.

But, getting back to the rain-ruined Test in Melbourne, it did have a silver lining as it led to the first one-day international played in Australia. Because the Melbourne cricket public had been denied Test play and partly because the washout had cost Australian cricket a small fortune, it was decided to play an Australia-England 50-overs match at the MCG the day after the rain dissipated.

Australia won by 23 runs, but the cricket world was the big winner as this one-off international proved that one-day cricket was the financial saviour the game had needed so desperately for years.

England eventually took a 1-0 lead in the 1970-1 Test series and I was dropped for the final Test, at the SCG. Naturally, I was shattered, but it at least gave me the opportunity to get into cricket broadcasting and I was behind the microphone for the ABC when all hell broke loose after Australian batsman Terry Jenner was hit on the head by a delivery from England pace man John Snow.

A drunken lout took his life in his own hands by grabbing Snow as the Englishmen went to field on the fine leg boundary. Snow, built like an Australian Rules centre half-back, could have broken the yob in two, but showed great restraint as beer cans whistled through the air.

Illingworth quite rightly took his team from the ground until order was restored and England went on to win the Test, the series and the Ashes.

It was quite an introduction to cricket broadcasting and I still wonder how the brave yob would have reacted had the powerful Snow challenged him to sort it out on the other side of the fence.

Snow reason to go

The mention of John Snow's name reminds me of how veteran English batsman Colin Cowdrey answered his country's call in 1974-5 when Australian fast bowlers Dennis Lillee and Jeff Thomson were terrorising the Poms.

England was in dire straights and desperately needed someone who could hold the batting together. The selectors therefore plumped for Cowdrey who, at that time, was 41 years of age and with nothing to prove to anyone at any level.

The selectors telephoned Cowdrey at his Kent home in the depth of the English winter. The great batsman was sitting in his dressing gown in front of a log fire when the telephone rang. It was, to say the least, an interesting conversation and Cowdrey was asked for a quick reply.

As soon as he replaced the receiver he looked out his lounge-room window and saw snow drifting from a leaden sky. The glorious county of Kent was a carpet of snow and Cowdrey decided there and then that even the ferocious heat of the Australian summer would be far preferable to the freezing cold of England.

He made himself available and, within days, was facing the twin torments of Lillee and Thomson. It was enough heat for any man to handle and although Cowdrey did not make big scores, he acquitted himself very well and bravely hooked the pace men to show that he still knew a thing or two about batting.

But, as Cowdrey later admitted, he might have done better to have chosen the snow of England instead of the heat from Lillee and Thomson.

Which reminds me of other Englishmen asked to tour Australia as stand-ins on the tours of Australia. One was the autocratic "Lord" Ted Dexter and the other an unfortunate spin bowler named John Mortimer (no, not the author of the same name who wrote the *Rumpole of the Bailey* books).

I say "unfortunate" because Mortimer not only was asked to bowl in 40 degree Celsius heat in Melbourne almost immediately after arriving in England, he also chucked up his lunch.

As for "Lord" Ted, he made an immediate impression and not only played well for England but confirmed his image as one of the game's aristocrats by turning up to cocktail parties in a white tuxedo jacket. He was very much the dapper English gentleman!

The V sign

Although Tests and one-day internationals are played in front of large crowds, there are times when a barracker's comment reaches the ears of those on the field. It seems that some barrackers wait for a deathly hush before letting fly with what sometimes is wit, but usually is nonsense.

I have heard them all, from "'Ave a go, ya mug" to "You couldn't bowl a hoop". However, one piece of barracking directed at me in a Test against England at the Gabba was extremely witty, even if a little unfair.

I was captaining Australia and doing my very best to winkle out the England batsmen when I decided to use Victorian Alan Connolly from one end and another Victorian in Bob Cowper from the other end.

The two sent down over after over and it finally was too much for one parochial Queenslander, who shouted: "Hey, Lawry, why don't you bowl (New South Welshman) John Gleeson? He has a grandmother who comes from Geelong."

I should have given the barracker the V-sign - V for Victoria, that is.

Far from the madding crowd

By now we all are familiar with the scenes when Australia wins an Ashes series in England...the Australians on a balcony and spraying champagne over all those silly enough to stand underneath...or leg-spinner Shane Warne gyrating in victory vigorously enough to have all those in the tomato sauce and mustard ties of the Marylebone Cricket Club choking on their gin and tonics.

Well, it is not a recent development as the Australian team of 1961 attempted a similar type of celebration. We had just defeated England in the Fourth Test at Old Trafford, Manchester, to retain the Ashes.

To say the least, it was an extraordinary Test win because England seemed certain to win mid-afternoon on the final day. However, excellent bowling from skipper Richie Benaud turned the tide Australia's way and team manager Syd Webb decided to celebrate with champagne.

The first problem was that we had to wait almost quarter of an hour for the champagne to arrive as it earlier had been sent to the England dressing room in anticipation of a Pommy victory.

When it did arrive, assistant manager Ray Steele suggested we move out to the balcony to celebrate our win with the crowd. You can imagine our surprise - and embarrassment - when we looked down and did not see a single fan.

That 1961 victory was years before flocks of Australians travelled to England, either as backpackers or in groups as cricket lovers. Never mind, the celebrations were just as sweet.

The lady in the sari

The 1969 Australian tour of India was extremely arduous, for all sorts of reasons. Not only did we have to contend with heat, dust and poor food, but almost every member of the tour party took ill and, to add to our worries, there were crowd riots.

Ian Chappell, in his book "Chappelli", perfectly described the conditions we experienced at Bombay when he wrote:

"The stadium-guesthouse where we stayed wasn't fit for a dog. One evening, some of the players looked for toasted sandwiches at the stadium. They were told that the cook had gone but there was some bread in the kitchen.

"Brian Taber went downstairs and came back with a loaf under his arm. 'If you want to eat another meal in this place, don't go down and look at the kitchen,' he said.

"Being curious, a couple of us went to investigate and we found cats in the refrigerator, cats running over the uncovered food, green slime on the floor, barred windows with no glass, and a rubbish tip with an unbelievable stench outside the window."

There were several incidents on this tour and, by the time we reached Bangalore for a match against the Western Zone, we had just about had enough. Then, to make matters worse, we played poorly and looked certain to be defeated.

I used every trick in the book in an effort to avoid defeat and, at one stage, even withdrew after complaining about a sari-clad woman who had walked in front of the sight-screen.

It all became too much for the fans and they rioted - but at least we avoided defeat.

Not out, not out, not out

It always pays to know the laws of cricket, as my Victorian teammate Lindsay Kline discovered in a match against South Australia at the Adelaide Oval.

Spinner Kline accidentally kicked the stumps over on his follow through and then went through what could only be described as a comic routine as he tried to affect a run out, with both batsmen stranded at one end.

Lindsay Kline -
in a spin

Kline picked up a stump and rubbed

the ball against it. Not out! He picked up and other stump and again rubbed the ball against it. Not out! He then picked up the third stump and rubbed the ball against it. Not out!

All this was hilarious enough but, with the two batsmen watching dumbfounded, Kline started rubbing the ball in the holes where the stumps had been. Not out!

What Kline should have done was to retrieve one of the stumps and place it in its hole and then remove it again with the ball. Oh well, we all live and learn!

Bill Lawry's
GREAT CRICKET JOKE BOOK

Tales from my many cricket friends

And here are just a few tales from my many cricket friends, just to prove that cricket really is a funny game.

Alan Hurst

A fine medium-fast bowler who could get quite a bit of movement, Alan Hurst made his Test debut for Australia against New Zealand in 1973-4 and went on to play 12 Tests. He played regularly for Victoria from 1972-80 and later established himself as a popular radio commentator.

Feet-first

Fans sitting in the old Bay 13 at the MCG loved their cricket and, in particular, their Victorian heroes. Top of their popularity chart when I first played for Victoria was Max Walker and, several years after I had retired from first-class cricket, they could not get enough of Merv Hughes.

Both Walker and Hughes played up to the boys (and some girls) in Bay 13 with considerable banter and plenty of skylarking. Walker almost always would urge the crowd to get behind the Australian - or Victorian - team, while everyone has seen how the fans imitated every Hughes movement during his warm-up exercises.

Playing in the same team as Walker presented me with some difficulties as I also was expected to have a rapport with the Bay 13 crowd. Although not as flamboyant as Mr Walker, I did have a lot of fun fielding in front of that particular section of the MCG crowd and did my very best to entertain them, cricket apart.

During one Test match I was offered a drink from a can of beer. I declined as politely as possible, but the bloke with the can refused to take no for an answer. It was a dilemma as persistent refusal could have led to a minor incident, especially as the man with the can obviously had consumed far too much of his swag of beer than was good for him.

On the other hand, it would not have looked good to be sipping alcohol while fielding. I therefore worked out a compromise with my beer-drinking friend, who, incidentally, was dressed only in shorts and thongs.

I explained as politely as possible why I could not drink the beer, but added that I would be extremely grateful if I could have some ice from his eskie. "No worries," he slurred, as he reached into his eskie and then handed me a slice of ice to quench my thirst.

The ice felt good as I pushed it around my mouth. It was an extremely hot day and the ice gave me some small relief...until I turned back to see the beer-drinker with his feet in the eskie.

I marched over to the fence and asked: "How long have you had your feet in the ice?"

"All bloody day," he replied. "How else do you think I keep cool in this bloody heat?"

You can rest assured I gave my mouth a good rinse during the tea break.

Keith Stackpole

A punishing opening batsman, Keith Stackpole made his Test debut against England in 1965-6 and was an Australian team stalwart for a decade. He played 43 Tests for 2807 runs at an average of 37.42.

The star professional

Just before I made my Test debut I was given the opportunity to play Lancashire League cricket with the Ramsbottom club and, even though the money was not all that flash, it represented an early opportunity to go to England to broaden my cricket horizon.

If my memory serves me right, the offer involved passage to England for my wife and I and little more than accommodation and living expenses. At the time of the offer I was just another Victorian cricketer and therefore in no bargaining position.

But, soon after signing the contract, I played two Tests for Australia and the Ramsbottom club congratulated itself on getting a highly-credentialled professional for next to nothing.

As soon as I arrived in England I went to the cricket suppliers and stocked up on bats, gloves and pads. After all, I was the team professional and I at least wanted to look the part.

Ramsbottom, an old mill town, was all I expected - full of warm-hearted people who really took to their cricket. As the team professional, I was welcomed everywhere and was always invited in for a cup of tea and cakes.

I was more than happy to involve myself in these social niceties as there was not much else to the town. After a bit of practice, there was little else to do than walk the streets and have a chat to the butcher, the baker, the candle-stick maker and all the people who would ask me about the next weekend's match.

However, all that changed very quickly after my first four innings realised scores of 0, 0, 8 and 0. I just could not take a trick and, all of a sudden, the butcher's door was closed, the baker wouldn't see me and the invitations to afternoon tea dried up.

It was almost panic stations as I desperately needed a big score to regain confidence. Otherwise, I could see myself being the laughing stock of Ramsbottom. Fortunately, I got a telephone call from a bloke named Ken Greives, a New South Welshman who had played County cricket with Lancashire and even played professional league soccer with the Stockport County club.

Ken told me I should get myself to Old Trafford to have a session in the nets on decent wickets. It sounded like good advice, so I accepted the invitation and even watched the touring West Indies play Lancashire.

The nets session helped restore some confidence but, best of all, Ken gave me some more than useful local advice. "Do you talk to the umpires before a match?" he asked.

This question was a puzzler as it was most unusual in Australia to talk to the umpires, so I shook my head from side to side in the negative.

"Well, next time you play go straight to their room and get them on your side," Ken advised me.

So, in my next match - against Todmorden - I was so desperate that I turned my back on old Australian habits to go into the umpires' room and have a chat.

"Hi," I greeted them. "I'm Keith Stackpole from Australia and it's good to meet you blokes."

They were chuffed and, after a bit of chit-chat, asked me about the standard of umpiring in the Lancashire League. I knew it was a leading question, so I blew up their tyres a little by suggesting that the standard was almost as good as in first-class cricket.

I could amost see their chests swell with pride and knew instantly that I had made an impression.

We won the toss and batted, my nerves jangling as another failure would have meant even greater embarrassment. Then, when on eight, I copped a short ball and tried to play it behind square. Instead, the ball sat up and hit my glove. A fraction of a second later I heard every member of the Todmorden team shout an appeal. I was gone. There was no way I would wriggle out of this.

I waited for what seemed an eternity and, finally, the umpire at the bowlers' end shook his head and said: "Not out." I felt like a man who had escaped the gallows and I wanted to kiss the umpire, especially as I knew damned well that I should have been given out.

I tickled the next ball around the corner for a single and, while I was leaning on my bat at the bowler's end, the umpire sidled up to me and said: "You got a touch to that one, didn't you?"

I was flabbergasted and could only reply: "Yeah, so why didn't you give me out?"

Without batting an eyelid, the umpire told me: "You don't seem like a bad bloke. I thought I'd give you a start."

I made only 34 that day, but it was enough to give me the shot of confidence I needed and I went on to top the Lancashire League batting aggregate that season. And I always made sure I popped into the umpires' room for a friendly chat before the start of play.

Another close call

I must admit that at the height of my time as an Australian representative I developed a feuding relationship with England's Tony Greig, who surely must have been one of the most aggressive and abrasive cricketers to represent the old enemy.

The feud went back to the time Australia played a series against the Rest of the World when a tour by South Africa was cancelled in 1971-2. During one of these "Tests" I was given out off a ball by Greig, caught by South African Hilton Ackerman.

It was in the last over of the day and I was convinced the ball did not carry. In fact, teammate Ian Chappell said to me: "It didn't look as if it carried." However, I accepted the umpire's decision - until I went to the opposition's rooms for a drink, where there were cries of "we did yer" and "gotcha".

Being a hot-headed bloke from Collingwood, I saw red as the inference was that they suspected I should not have been given out. And, because Greig was the bowler and one of the dressing room ringleaders, I had him in my sights.

Just a few months later I was with the Australian team in England and playing a match against Greig's County, Sussex, and I was determined he would never again have the better of me, no matter what he might say or do.

I opened the batting against a formidable combination in Greig and John Snow and, very early, a Snow leg-cutter removed my off stump. In normal circumstances I would have marched off without a thought, but I stood there fuming as Greig had bellowed an appeal for what seemed like five or 10 seconds. I thought this was over the top, especially as the off stump was sent cart-wheeling and there was absolutely no need for any appeal.

Greig had needled me and, when I took block for the second innings, I was determined to make a big score. I put my head down and concentrated as if my life depended on a mountain of runs.

My resolution paid off and I reached 96 without too many difficulties. I desperately wanted the century, even if only to stick it up Greig. But when batting partner Paul Sheahan stroked a ball from Mike Buss, I found myself in terrible trouble.

Sheahan, a Geelong College product with a cut-glass accent, shouted something like "Yaaas". I tore down the wicket, but well aware that Greig was fast moving in on the ball from mid-on.

Sheahan also spotted quick movement in the field and, as Greig's huge left hand reached out, my batting partner had second thoughts about taking the single. "Go back," he shouted, and tore back down the wicket like a startled gazelle.

Sheahan, lean and lithe, was an athletics champion at school and had no problems making his ground. On the other hand, I looked like a baby elephant trying to reach sanctuary. My bum cheeks must have wobbled like jelly as I pushed myself down the wicket.

I can still see the ball in Greig's hand, cocked for throwing, and, from the other eye, umpire Cec Pepper in perfect position to make a decision. I pushed myself even harder to avoid the humiliation of being run out by Greig just four runs short of a century.

I failed by a good metre and a half. Greig's throw scattered the stumps and all I could hear was this braying from my jubilant adversary. I knew I was out, especially as the braying went on and on.

After following through on my run, I turned and saw Pepper still leaning over as if trying to make a decision. You can imagine my relief when he finally unbent himself and said: "Not out."

I couldn't believe my ears, and nor could Greig. As I played Joe Cool, trying to pretend that I always knew I had made my ground, Greig went ballistic. He grabbed Pepper by the coat and shouted: "You bastard; he was out by a bloody mile. He must have been out."

Pepper merely brushed Greig's hands aside, patted his coat and sniffed: "If you don't back off, I'll report you."

Greig stomped away fuming and, as Pepper replaced the stumps, turned to me and said: "It's your lucky day. If it had been anyone else but that bastard you would be back in the pavilion."

Method in my madness

I was playing Melbourne District cricket with Carlton against University one day and, as I made my way to the wicket to open the batting with Bill Tyson, I could not help but reflect that it was the most glorious of days. Even better, the wicket was an absolute belter and I drooled at the prospect of a feast of runs.

Unfortunately, however, my impetuosity got the better of me in the very first over. I called for a quick single and ran out Tyson even before he had faced a ball. It was a batsman's worst nightmare and Carlton was 1/0.

I knuckled down to make amends and, by stumps, John Scholes (now Victoria's coach) and I had taken the score to 1/340 and I was well-pleased with myself - until Tyson confronted me in the dressing room.

"Thanks for running me out," he spat, poking a finger in my chest.

I had to think fast to make light of the situation and then came up with a reply that left Tyson speechless. "The wicket was such a good one I had to make sure I got Scholes in as early as possible," I told him tongue in cheek.

And, thankfully, Tyson burst out laughing.

Flash Gordon

I often have been asked to nominate the fastest bowler I have faced and my answer always takes everyone by surprise. Gordon Rorke, who played just four Tests for Australia in the late '60s, deserved a much better record as his career was ruined by a bout of hepatitis.

Rorke also had a long "drag" in his follow-through and, with a different "no-ball rule" in those days, it often meant facing him from less than the full distance of the pitch - a terrifying prospect considering Rorke's pace.

I had never faced Rorke when I opened the batting for Victoria with Ian Redpath in a match against New South Wales at the SCG and had no idea of just how much pace Rorke could generate. Sure, I had heard the big blond bowler was quick, but had to learn the hard way.

As usual, Redders offered me the opportunity to take strike and I accepted, much to my regret. After taking block, I looked around the field and licked my lips. There were five slips, two gullies and two other fielders in an arc that looked like the Great Wall of China.

There was only one man forward of point and I should have known the field placings had been set because of Rorke's great bowling pace. On the other hand, I thought I was being laid a run picnic. How naive of me!

Rorke ran his fingers through his hair and tore in like a demented bull. As he got closer, he looked bigger and bigger and meaner and meaner. In fact, by the time he had rolled his arm over I thought he was going to shirt-front me.

The ball fairly whizzed past my ear and thudded into the gloves of NSW 'keeper Doug Ford, who was standing further back than normal. The crowd whistled at this sizzling delivery and I had to take a deep breath. "God, this bloke really is bloody quick," I told myself.

Yet there was worse! When I looked down to the other end of the pitch, I saw Redders killing himself laughing. He knew I had been beaten by sheer pace and was absolutely rapt to be watching my agony while he safely squatted on his bat at the other end.

"You rotten bugger," I thought to myself. "I'll get you." And I did!

I somehow managed to see out the next few balls and, on the second last ball of the over, hooked the ball - straight over Rorke's head. Now I must admit that I had intended to hook to fine leg but, instead, the ball was so quick I mis-timed the shot and it went straight.

I knew the ball would not go to the boundary, but there were four runs in the shot anyway. However, I ambled through the first couple of runs to make sure we ran only three - so that Redders would have to face the next express delivery from Rorke.

I then watched from the other end as Redders' Adam's apple revved up and down like a piston while he waited for the final delivery in Rorke's first over. It was his turn to suffer and my turn to laugh.

But, credit where credit is due. Redders, a tremendously courageous opening batsman, went on to make a century. I got only 30 or so, but I at least had got my own back on my batting partner.

Sam Trimble

One of the best cricketers never to play a Test for Australia, Sam Trimble had a remarkable record for Queensland, playing 122 games for his State from 1959-75. A hard-hitting batsman, he also was a useful change bowler.

Defying the odds

Soon after I made my Sheffield Shield debut for Queensland I had my confidence shattered when a spectator at the Gabba yelled out to me: "Hey Trimble, you can't bat, you can't bowl and you can't field. Is one of the selectors your uncle?"

Of course, I did my very best to prove him wrong but was still feeling my way a match or two later when playing against Victoria. The 'keeper, and I shall not embarrass him by naming him, squatted over the stumps and snarled at me as I settled nervously into my innings: "You are the worst batsman I have ever seen."

I somehow managed to survive long enough to score a century and, as I doffed my cap, I turned to the 'keeper and snapped: "Not bad for being the worst batsman, eh?"

But, getting back to my original tormentor, I could have done with an uncle as a selector on the Australian tour of the West Indies in 1965. I was the touring team's third opener, with Bill Lawry and Bob Simpson, the regular Test openers. And both were tour selectors.

It was a fantastic trip as we not only had a great time - socially and cricket-wise in the Caribbean, but also visited San Francisco and New York. In fact, I remember Bill and I stopping at Macey's department store in New York and buying our wives identical yellow outfits. They were very skimpy and, on reflection, might have been bought because we had been away for three months.

Later in my career I captained the 1970 Australian "B" team to New Zealand while Bill captained the "A" team to South Africa. My touring party included a very young Greg Chappell and, although he was disappointed not to be with the Test party, I told him it probably was a blessing in disguise as South Africa white-washed Australia in that series and Greg got his chance at Test level less than 12 months later.

Ray Jordon

A lively wicketkeeper with great technique and good foot-work, Ray Jordon toured India and South Africa with Australian teams and was unlucky not to have played Test cricket. A Victorian stalwart, he was his State's 'keeper for almost a decade from 1966.

You won't get me

I was playing in the Victorian side against South Australia at the MCG in the late '60s when skipper Bill Lawry got himself into a bad case of the jitters about running between the wickets when close to a century. The closer Lawry got to three figures, the more erratic were his calls for quick singles and, at one stage, he looked as if he would run out of batting partners.

He ran Ian Redpath out by half the length of the pitch and, when Paul Sheahan went in to bat, we warned him to watch out for Lawry's calls. "No worries," Sheahan replied. "He won't get me."

Less than 15 minutes later, Sheahan was back in the dressing-room after being run out following an optimistic Lawry call. Next man in was Les Joslin, who also proudly insisted: "He won't get me." Half an hour later, Joslin was back in the dressing room after being stranded more than halfway down the pitch.

Next man in was Peter Bedford, the champion South Melbourne footballer who was unlucky not to have won Test selection. Bedford also insisted he would not fall to a bad Lawry call but he, at least, had a large section of a very vocal crowd on his side.

Bedford, a tally clerk on Melbourne's wharves, had no sooner taken block for his first ball than a huge section of the crowd of about 15,000 started heckling Lawry and more than one of them shouted: "If you run Bedford out we'll burn your bloody house down."

We learned later that these comments came from a group of wharfies who had gone to the MCG to support their work-mate, Bedford. Lawry did not have to worry as Bedford survived until Lawry had made his ton and then declared the Victorian innings closed.

You're next...

One of my worst experiences in first-class cricket was being thumped on the jaw by a rising delivery from Western Australia's Laurie Mayne in a match at the WACA. I knew immediately I was in trouble and, in fact, was rushed to hospital with a broken jaw.

This was bad enough but, when my Victorian teammates visited me that evening, they told me how brilliant Peter Bedford had been in deputising for me. In fact, they rubbed it in by telling me of how Bedford had made a particularly brilliant stumping. It was only later that I learned the ball had hit him on the pads and then cannoned into the stumps.

Although I felt as if someone had fired a bullet into my head, I was released from hospital the next morning. My head swathed in bandages, I made my way to the WACA to see how my teammates were going in their chase for Victory and was horrified when team captain Bill Lawry ordered me to pad up as I was next to bat.

"You must be joking," I mumbled. "I'm as crook as a dog."

"We're losing wickets and you'll have to bat if necessary," Lawry insisted.

I shook as I watched the Victorian batsmen defy the Sandgropers and, believe me, I had never been so supportive of my teammates' performances. Then, after an hour or so, a wicket fell.

I must admit I almost lost my nerve and started looking for somewhere to hide. However, I could feel Lawry's eyes boring into me as I rose to my feet. Then, at the very last second, he put a hand on my shoulder and said: "Don't worry, we'll send someone else in to bat."

Fortunately, my teammates held on so that I did not have to bat and to this day I am convinced Lawry was only winding me up. But, boy, he certainly did a mighty fine job in getting me to as close to panic as I have ever been in my life.

Incidentally, I faced up to Mayne the next year and went through mental and physical agony as he gave me a good working over. I got hit from pillar to post and, just a couple of overs into my innings, I decided to abandon my usual practice of batting bareheaded.

I called for my Victorian cloth cap. Mind you, this was in an era before helmets, but what protection would a cotton cap have given me if speedster Mayne again whacked me on the noggin? None at all, but it certainly made me feel a lot more comfortable.

The law of averages

I had such a good time with the bat - mainly through being not out in most innings - on the 1969-70 tour of South Africa that by the time we reached Cape Town for the last match I was just ahead of Bill Lawry on the tour batting averages.

This was no mean feat, as Lawry was the star opening batsman and the tour captain, while I was a struggling reserve wicketkeeper who batted mainly down the order. Nevertheless, I was quite chuffed with the idea of returning to Australia at the top of the batting averages.

The only problem was that in that final match in Cape Town I was dismissed early, while Lawry went to a make quite a big score. This meant I now headed the averages by only the tiniest of margins.

Would you believe that Lawry sent me in to bat early in the second innings and, of course, I was dismissed very cheaply - with Lawry heading the averages. To this day I am convinced it was a Lawrry ruse and, knowing his cunning as a cricket captain, I would not put it past him.

Lawry, despite criticism often levelled at him for being a slow batter and a relatively conservative skipper, was in a no-win situation late in his Test career as he often was forced to bat slowly and cautiously to protect fragile batting line-ups.

For example, when Lawry took over as Victorian captain in 1961 the side lost many matches within three days and former Australian great Ken Miller, in a nationally syndicated cricket column, suggested Victoria was the worst Sheffield Shield side he had seen.

I believe this criticism not only hurt Lawry but stung him into great efforts of concentration to get his sides through difficulties.

His slow batting earned him the nickname "the corpse in pads" but this was grossly unfair and, in fact, Lawry was a marvellously dedicated cricketer with immense powers of concentration.

Mr Magoo's substitute

Victorian cricketer Ian Law, who played only a handful of games for his State, was better known as a champion Victorian Football League (now AFL) rover with the Hawthorn club. Known as Mr Magoo because of his poor eyesight, Law was a bit of a laid-back character, as reflected by an incident when he was twelfth man for Victoria in a match against South Australia at the MCG in the '60s.

South Australia was batting, with Les Favell hooking and cutting everything in sight. He was making an absolute mess of the Victorian attack and there seemed little we could do about it...until fate intervened.

One of the Victorian fieldsmen had to leave the ground for a minor injury and the message went back to the dressing room for Law to take the field. However, the laid-back Law did not have his cricket boots on and was nowhere near ready to take the field.

Instead, South Australian twelfth man Neil Hawke volunteered to take the field for Victoria. When play resumed, Favell continued his attack and skied a massive hit to square leg. Hawke, an extremely athletic cricketer who also was a star footballer, took off and, with a mighty leap at least a metre off the ground, took a truly magnificent catch in his right hand.

It was an extraordinary situation, with South Australia's star batsman caught by a teammate. Favell, a grumpy customer at the best of times, could only stand and glare at Hawke, who did not know whether to celebrate his marvellous catch or run for cover.

Finally, after what seemed an eternity, Favell snarled: "I'll see you in the rooms."

I would have loved to have been a fly on the wall in the SA rooms that afternoon.

Greg Chappell

An elegant batsman with a flawless technique, Greg Chappell made his Test debut against England in 1970-1 and then established himself as one of Australia's cricket greats. He succeeded his brother Ian as Australian captain.

The <u>real</u> Bill Lawry

The recordings by Billy Birmingham in imitation of the Channel Nine cricket commentary team have been enormously popular, even with the commentators themselves. And none more so than Bill Lawry, even though Phanto is the brunt of most of "The Twelfth Man's" jokes.

In fact, there was a time when Lawry liked nothing better than to parody the parody and could not wait to imitate colleague Richie Benaud in the commentary box. Then, in a Mercantile Mutual Cup match between Tasmania and Queensland at Hobart, Lawry got his big chance.

The Tasmanians reached 2/222 and, as anyone who has heard *The Twelfth Man* tapes would know, this particular scoreline is a Benaud AND Birmingham favorite. Benaud always manages to roll the "twos" and the brilliant Birmingham always imitates him perfectly.

Lawry just could not help himself this particular day, despite Benaud's revered and almost untouchable position among the Nine commentators. Lawry rolled his "twos' in giving the score and, in fact, it easily could have been Benaud doing the commentary.

The only problem was that Lawry thought it was so funny he could not make any further comment. Every time he opened his mouth he fell backwards laughing and had to put the microphone in his lap. And, with Benaud reduced to stony silence, it probably was the only time an over televised on Nine went without commentary.

The real Twelfth Man

My first call-up to the Australian side was for the First Test against England at the Gabba in 1970. Also in the Australian side for the first time for that Test were Terry Jenner and Rod Marsh.

Now, we all knew Marsh was selected to keep wicket, but who was going to be twelfth man - Jenner or myself? I almost worried myself sick over what the selectors had in mind for that Test as, naturally, I was desperately keen to make my debut. However, I knew I would have to be patient as tradition decreed no-one would be told until just before the start of play.

We practised at the Gabba the day before the Test and, after a fairly heavy session, went to lunch at the Cricketers' Club. The training had built up my hunger and, sitting opposite Jenner, I reached out for a bread roll from a basket on the table. Precisely at the same moment, Jenner tried to do the same - with a fork.

ARGH!

As the fork came down, it struck me on the back of the hand, taking out quite a chunk. After a bit of yelping, I told Jenner to be more careful as I had to protect my hands.

You can imagine my shock and horror when Australian captain Bill Lawry quickly intervened: "I wouldn't worry if I was you, Greg." It was then - a day early - that I knew I would be carrying the drinks.

Geoff Lawson

A lion-hearted bowler who served Australia well over many years, Geoff Lawson made his Test debut against New Zealand in 1980-1 and did not bow out of the international scene until a decade later. He played 46 Tests and took 180 wickets at an average of 30.56.

Practice makes perfect

I was one of the Nine commentators during the 1993 Australian tour of England and learned first-hand just how much effort goes into bringing viewers the very best commentory and pictures.

The first morning of any Test match always is a very exciting time and the adrenalin got to me an hour or so before the first ball was bowled in the Test at Trent Bridge during that 1993 season.

There was not a cloud in the sky, the larks were singing and all was well with the world. I just could not wait to get behind the microphone, expect that I knew I would not be involved in the televising of the first half hour or so as this honor almost always went to Bill Lawry and Tony Greig.

I therefore meandered to the Nine commentory box, known affectionately as "The Potting Shed", and then sat outside in the sun reading a newspaper. I was so relaxed I almost fell asleep, only to be told 10 minutes before the scheduled start of play that I had to get behind the microphone as Greig had been delayed getting to the ground.

More excited than ever, I stepped into "The Potting Shed" and heard a familiar voice. My God, I thought, the Test already has started - without me. Lawry was calling the match ball by ball and, to pinch his famous expression, it was all happening. From what I had heard, a wicket already had fallen, and I had missed it.

I reached for my microphone but, on looking out on the ground, realised that the teams had yet to take the field. Lawry merely was practising and totally focused on the job ahead. It was a lesson in broadcasting professionalism and reflected his genuine love of the game and his pivotal role with Channel Nine.

Well %$#* said

It is not uncommon for a fast bowler to mutter the odd expletive during the course of a match. And, of course, some are better at cursing than others, with Merv Hughes near the top of the class.

I was playing in a County match with the Australian touring team when I heard the following exchange:

Merv, to the batsman: "What sort of $%^* shot is that?"

Merv, to the other batsman: "You were $%^* lucky that time."

Merv, to the first batsman: "Ill get you next $%^* ball."

Then, as Merv completed the over, the umpire turned to him and said: "And that, gentlemen, completes another $%^* over."

Kim Hughes

A wonderfully talented batsman, Kim Hughes made his debut for Western Australia in 1975-6 and eventually played 70 Tests for a batting aggregate of 4415 at an average of 37.41. He also captained Australia.

The perfect duck

As a junior cricketer, my coach - Frank Parry - had absolute faith in my batting ability. In fact, he used to drive people mad by suggesting that I was the next big thing and that I one day would captain Australia.

It was all very flattering, but there were times when I found it very difficult to live up to his expectations. In fact, I had a very lean period when I was about 16 years of age and made three consecutive ducks. I could not score a run to save my soul and, after the third failure, went home in a depressed state of mind.

My father, a headmaster, could read boys and asked me: "What's wrong?"

No sooner had I told him that I again had failed to score, the telephone rang. It was Parry, who said: "How are you, champ?"

He always called me champ, but this time it grated. Champ? I felt more like a chump and told him so.

To my amazement, Parry replied: "Don't worry, champ. I have seen Bradman and I have seen Harvey, the best there have been and I know a good batsman when I see one. You are moving your feet well and you are getting right behind the ball. In fact, your duck today was the best I have ever seen."

I could not believe my ears. My coach didn't regard me as a failure after all. There was still some joy to life. The end of the world was not nigh. I therefore had a smile on my face as I returned to the family dinner table.

Dad turned to me and asked me: "What did Frank say?"

I replied: "He told me it was the best duck he had ever seen."

Dad chewed over this before commenting: "You're both idiots."

My coach's comments were designed to keep me positive and they worked. I went to bed that night convinced that you can have success even when you are failing. His philosophy provided me with the attitude that no-one should fear failure.

And I always chuckle at how I had made the best duck he had ever seen.

David Saker

A fine all-rounder with the knack of producing wickets or a big score when needed, David Saker is a current member of the Victorian Sheffield Shield squad.

Well, you have a go

When I first broke in the Victorian squad I was selected to play for the State's second eleven against the ACT in Canberra and all went well when we made 400-plus in the first innings. Our problems started when we had to bowl to champion West Indies opener Gordon Greenidge on a flat track.

One of the most attacking batsmen of his era, Greenidge threatened to take us apart. He had all the guile of a Test veteran and the strength of an ox. However, my Victorian teammate Peter Smith, a bit of a character, managed to beat him with a superb delivery and was convinced he had trapped the great man lbw.

We all roared an appeal as this was the one batsman we just had to dismiss cheaply. But, after a long deliberation, the umpire shook his head from side to side in the negative, even though we all thought it was plumb.

Smith, who was more convinced than any of us that Greenidge should have been given out, was so infuriated he tossed the ball back to the umpire and snapped: "If you think that's not out, you can bowl to him."

That little outburst cost Smith a "stern warning", but he felt it was worth it as Greenidge went on to make something like 160 not out. At one stage late in Greenidge's innings, Smith turned to me and said: "Watch this; it will be very interesting."

Smith tore in and sent down a shortish delivery just outside leg stump. It was the type of delivery commentators describe as "fruit for the sideboard". Greenidge made the most of the offer by cutting the ball magnificently and imperiously to the boundary.

As Smith made his way to his bowling mark, I asked him: "What was going to be so interesting?"

"Oh," Smith replied. "I just wanted to show you how well he could cut. Great shot, wasn't it?"

Shaun Graf

A multi-talented cricketer, Shaun Graf was unlucky not to win Test selection, especially as he was twelfth man for two Tests and played one-day internationals for Australia. A strong medium-fast bowler, he also was a punishing batsman for Victoria over many seasons.

Always in the middle

As a Victorian selector, I sat with Bill Lawry during a tight Sheffield Shield match at the Junction Oval, Melbourne, during the 1990-1 season when the Vics last won the trophy. Bill, as always, got caught up in the excitement of the match and could hardly sit still.

Bill always has worn his heart on his sleeve when it comes to Victorian cricket and I learned first hand how he rode every ball, every run, every wicket in every Victorian match and, at one stage in this particular match, he jumped to his feet and shouted: "He's out...oh, no he's not...oh, he is."

I turned to Bill and said: "Gee, I'd hate to have played in the same side as you and shared the rooms while you were waiting to bat."

Without batting an eyelid, Bill turned to me and said: "I was never much in the rooms, son."

Incidentally, as a young cricketer I knew I really had made it in the Victorian team when Bill started calling me by my correct Christian name. For at least two years he had been calling me "Shane".

However, that was typical of Bill, who always seemed to get his names mixed up. I can recall the day we were discussing football and Bill suggested "that Geelong bloke, Gary Albert, was a good footballer". Of course, Bill was referring to the great Gary Ablett.

Tony Greig

A marvellously competitive all-rounder, Tony Greig learned his cricket skills in his native South Africa, but moved to England and later captained the England Test side.

The homing instinct

It is well known that Bill Lawry is a great pigeon fancier. Always has been, always will be. But what generally is not known is that Bill's hobby for years kept him from moving house.

After all, keeping homing pigeons makes it extremely difficult to pull up roots as the birds just keep returning to their old home. And who in their right mind would want to buy a pigeon fancier's home unless every step was taken to beat the homing instinct?

Bill, wife Joy and family settled down to a quiet, contented life in the humble outer northern Melbourne suburb of Reservoir.

Bill, a very much down to earth sort of bloke, probably could have afforded to move into a much more salubrious suburb, but it just was not his style. Then, of course, what would he do with his pigeons?

Finally, however, Bill and Joy bit the bullet and moved into a semi-rural retreat on the outskirts of Melbourne. It was a big shift, in more ways than one as it meant culling Bill's beloved coop.

This was a hell of a problem as killing birds is never a pleasant task. But it just had to be done and Bill had to start his pigeon breeding process all over again to prevent the older pigeons returning to his former home and driving the new owners insane.

Bill kept only a few breeding pigeons, but now is right back in the swings of things in terms of pigeon-racing, with yours truly - believe it or not - as one of his partners in a big international venture.

Now, contrary to public perception, Bill and I have an excellent relationship and, in fact, are very good mates. We might appear to antagonise each other during our television commentaries and, although we might disagree on certain cricket matters, that's as far it goes.

Bill, after starting his pigeon breeding process all over again, realised that this was the perfect opportunity to cash in on his hobby - big-time. He learned there was a race in South Africa worth US$1 million dollars to the owner of the winning pigeon. And that's a lot of bird-seed in anyone's language.

The only problem for Bill was the cost of getting a couple of pigeons to South Africa and keeping them there for the million-dollar race. You can imagine my surprise when, on my 50th birthday, the postman delivered a most unusual parcel.

I could not believe my eyes when I removed the wrapping. There, delicately placed in a carefully-built nest, were two pigeon eggs. Accompanying them was a note wishing me a happy birthday, but also suggesting that I now could start breeding pigeons.

Then, just a few days later, I received an instruction manual on pigeon breeding. My starter's kit, courtesy of my mate Bill Lawry, was complete. And, just a few days later, Bill called me to tell me about the million-dollar bird race in South Africa.

Bill, as careful with his money as any Scot, wanted to know if I would be part of his pigeon-racing syndicate. And, after listening to him describe how we would spend the million dollars, I was hooked.

We now have two pigeons in South Africa being prepared for the big race. One of the pigeons is a strong, powerful-looking bird and even someone who would not know a pigeon from a sparrow could tell that this bird was bred in the purple. It is a magnificent looking specimen.

The other pigeon, I must admit, looks more like a cross-breed. If it were a dog, it would be called a mongrel. It is skinny, has barely enough feathers to cover its body and God knows how it finds its way home.

But I somehow have the feeling that if we do win the million bucks, it will be with the funny-looking bird with the hungry glint in its eye.

Ian Meckiff

Sadly, Ian Meckiff's career was cut short when he was called for throwing in a Test against South Africa in 1963. A left-arm pace bowler, he played 18 Tests for Australia and took 45 wickets at an average of 31.62.

Gunned down

Much has been said and written about the time I was "chucked out" of cricket in 1963. Briefly, umpire Col Egar called me for

Ian Meckiff - "chucked" out

throwing four times in my first over in the First Test against South Africa at the Gabba, Brisbane. Australian captain Richie Benaud had no option but to remove me from the bowling.

Naturally, the "throwing" incident created huge headlines around the world and it undoubtedly was the worst period of my life. My cricket career came to a shuddering stop while everyone from Adelaide to Alice Springs debated whether I had been treated fairly or not.

I was delighted that so many Australian cricket fans got behind me, but not so pleased when I heard that death threats had been made against both Egar and Benaud. This was most un-Australian and, as far as I was concerned, I just wanted the Test over and done with so that I could settle back and think about my future.

Australian teammate Bill Lawry, however, came up with one of the best practical jokes ever pulled in a cricket dressing room. Lawry, on the last day of the Test, convinced team masseur Jock Anderson to disguise himself and pretend to get even with skipper Benaud for taking me out of the Australian attack.

Anderson, in an old overcoat with the collar pulled up around his face, knocked on the dressing-room door on the final day and asked if he could see Benaud. Then, when the Australian skipper approached him, the heavily disguised Anderson produced a copy of the *Sporting Globe* and pointed to an article written by Ian McDonald.

This article posed the question: Why didn't Benaud bowl me from the other end? "Well," Anderson demanded. "What do have to say about this suggestion?"

Benaud had just opened his mouth to reply when Anderson produced what the skipper thought was a revolver, and fired.

Benaud turned white and often has said later that his life flashed before his eyes. The "revolver", however, was nothing more than a starting pistol.

Benaud still had his hand over his heart as Lawry headed for the door and into the rain (the day's play eventually was washed out), and he was killing himself laughing. God knows what would have happened had Benaud caught him.

Feed him to the vultures

Anyone who has played cricket at a serious level in Pakistan knows that conditions can be extremely difficult. Not only do visiting teams have to contend with unusual food and the lack of alcohol, (it is a Muslim country), but the standard of umpiring can leave a lot to be desired.

I toured Pakistan with the Australian team in 1959 and learned first hand just how difficult it was to get a leg before wicket decision against the local Test team. Umpires refused to even consider the possibility that a Pakistan batsman might have been plumb in front. On the other hand, the finger always was poised when the ball thudded into an Australian batsman's pad.

The First Test of the 1959 series was played at Dacca (now Bangladesh) and although Australian pace man Ray Lindwall bowled his heart out on a matting wicket placed over what was little more than rolled mud, he just could not get an lbw decision to go his way.

We all thought that Lindwall three times, at least, should have been given lbw decisions, but nothing would sway the umpires and we finally conceded that the only way to get a leg before wicket decision was to get the ball to run under the matting.

Sitting in the stands watching the match was Australian tour manager and former Test all-rounder Sam Loxton, a man who always has spoken his mind. Surrounded by the generals, colonels and air vice-marshalls of the ruling Pakistan junta (the country was under martial law at that time), Loxton gave vent to his feelings.

With tour medical officer Dr Ian McDonald and broadcaster Michael Charlton listening in amazement, Loxton pointed to a huge flock of scavenger-like kites flying overhead and told the assembled military brass: "See those birds up there. They're not kites; they're vultures. And the umpire's got to be dead."

Paul Reiffel

A big-hearted performer with claims of being a genuine all-rounder, Victorian Paul Reiffel had an excellent 1997 tour of England after originally missing the squad and flying in as a late replacement.

Bradman, the twelfth man

One of the more pleasant aspects of being selector for cricket tours is being able to sample the local hospitality. This was particularly true when I toured South Africa with an Australian side. The hosts went out of their way to ensure we sampled the local food and drink and, believe me, South African wines are excellent.

We visited the wineries in the area around Boland, not far from Cape Town, early in the tour and then played a match against the local first-class side.

Unfortunately for Boland, it somehow went into the match with an injured player who could not bat because of a broken finger. Because nothing was swinging on this match we agreed that the twelfth man could bat, and it was obvious very early that he was way out of form.

I must admit I gave him a hard time as I was trying to push my Test credentials with every possible wicket on tour. I sent down a ball that thudded into his gloves and he winced in pain. Next ball whistled around his ears and the third ball rapped him on the arm.

Finally, after he was belted black and blue over the course of my over, I turned to him and suggested: "You should have been content with just carrying the drinks."

To which he replied: "What do you expect from a twelfth man? Don Bradman?"

Allan Border

One of the great batsmen of the modern era, Allan Border made his first-class debut for NSW in 1977 and later moved to Queensland. He made his Test debut against England in 1978-9 and was appointed Australian captain in the summer of 1984-5. He established himself as one of Australia's great cricket captains and guided Australia to a World Cup triumph in 1987 and an Ashes series win over England in 1989. Border played 156 Tests for a batting average of 50.56, with a highest score of 205.

In the lions' den

Playing for Australia against England at the WACA in 1979, I had an experience I would prefer to forget, in more ways than one. And it all stemmed from the fact that it was the first time I had played at that ground as a member of the "home" team. Naturally, when I had represented NSW against Western Australia at the WACA I always had been in the "visitors'" room.

Australia's big adversary at that time was brilliant all-rounder Ian Botham, one of the most competitive cricketers the game has seen. Botham's appeals as a bowler usually were long and loud and, if the decision went against him when he genuinely thought the batsman should have been given out, he would stand and glare.

During the First Test of the 1979-80 series Botham all but went purple in the face when he thought I should have been given out. You can imagine his frustration - and fury - when the umpire turned down his appeal.

Naturally, I just stared down the wicket as if nothing had happened and, I suppose, Botham interpreted this as being cocky. He stormed back to his mark and whistled one down around my ear-hole. Then, with his very next ball, he rapped me on the pads and his appeal was louder and longer than ever.

Botham was almost beside himself with joy when I was given out, for just four runs. I was furious with myself as I had been given a let-off just two balls earlier and had not made the most of it. Worst of all, however, was that Botham had taken my wicket.

I marched angrily from the ground and into the rooms. I threw down my gloves and hurled my bat across the room. To be honest,

Allan Border - heroic stand

there were more than a few expletives - until I heard one or two cricketers tittering. It was then I realised I had walked into the England rooms. I had forgotten that I was supposed to be in the home team's rooms.

I high-tailed it out of the England rooms as fast as I could, especially after I heard England keeper David Bairstow laughing his head off. Then, to make matters worse, my Aussie teammates gave me hell when I eventually turned up in their room.

My only consolation was that Australia won the Test. So what's that they say about he who laughs last, etc.?

The worriers and the watchers

One of the most famous Ashes clashes was the Fourth Test of the 1982-3 series and I was in the thick of all the drama, along with Australian fast bowler Jeff Thomson. To say the least, the finish to this Test was extraordinary and although the cricket public sweated on every delivery as Australia tried to steal victory, it was nothing compared to the tension in the Australian rooms.

The background to this drama is that Australia needed 292 runs in its second innings for victory. Unfortunately, however, the ninth wicket fell for 218, leaving us 78 runs shy of the target with just over a day to play.

Although Thommo always showed enormous courage on the cricket field, the last thought on my mind as he strode to join me in the middle was that we would knock off the runs. It looked an extremely forlorn task, and the Englishmen knew it. They just wanted to get it over and done with so they could sip champagne as victors.

However, Thommo defied all the odds to stay with me to stumps. We had knocked off 41 of the required total but, despite my enormous admiration of Thommo's fighting spirit, I still did not contemplate victory. It seemed so far, far away, with a hell of a lot of work in front of us.

Then, when Thommo and I had a bit of a hit before play on the final day, we looked around and saw fans pouring into the MCG. I thought to myself: "Hey, these people are here in the hope we can perform some form or miracle. Thommo and I agreed not to let them down and decided that, no matter what, we at least would go down fighting.

The atmosphere was electric and Thommo and I were delighted with the crowd's faith in us, especially when they shouted out "good luck" or "you can do it" as we left the ground after our little practice session.

As we went into to bat, I told Thommo: "Let's get stuck in here. We'll fight every inch of the way, and, who knows?" When play resumed, there was an enormous roar. There might have been just 18,000 fans at the "G" that day, but the din was deafening. It gave us great encouragement.

Our plan, as usually the case in these cirumstances, was to protect the tail-end batsman. I therefore tried to take most of the strike, with the English field closing in at the end of each over to try and prevent this.

The runs came slowly but, the longer we were in the middle, the more convinced I was we could do it. Just 20 more, then only 10 to go. It was nailbiting stuff and I could barely watch when Thommo was on strike.

He did a superb job in holding up his end and, in fact, no tail-ender could have been more courageous. England was frustrated by Thommo's defiance but, with just three runs required for an Australian victory, Ian Botham struck the telling blow.

He got one to bounce a little more and Thommo edged the ball to Chris Tavare at second slip. My heart was in my mouth as Tavare clutched at the ball and, for a split second, I thought there had been a reprieve.

The ball bobbled out of Tavare's hands, only for Geoff Miller to dive and take the ball before it hit the ground. Thommo was out when we were just three runs short of victory. It was the 103rd ball of the day's play and we had come so far only to miss out by such a narrow margin.

Although fans around the world watched the drama on television or listened on radio, they missed out on another drama away from the wicket. If only there had been a television camera in the Australian dressing rooms!

As Thommo and I progressed the innings late on the fourth day, the Australian camp broke into two groups and, to understand this, I must describe the dressing room set-up at the MCG as there are two separate areas - one upstairs where members of the team can watch play, and the other downstairs where there is no viewing area.

It seems that late on the fourth day those who sat upstairs could barely watch play, while those downstairs were mainly the superstitious ones who did not want to know what was happening outside.

And, when play resumed the next day, everyone took the same positions - whether upstairs or downstairs - to avoid putting a mozz on Thommo and myself. It seems that as play progressed on the morning of the fifth day, the tensions in the two areas became almost unbearable.

The blokes upstairs were crying out "oh, he's out, no he's not" or "for heaven's sake, Thommo, go back" or "take the single, take the single". Downstairs, however, there was at least one card school and more than one comment to those upstairs to "keep it quiet".

This had nothing to do with team loyalties or patriotism, but more to do with the state of their battered nerves. They literally did not want to know, in case it was bad news out in the middle.

I have been told that one or two players sipped cans of beer throughout the agonising wait for either victory or defeat and, according to those in the rooms, it was a madhouse of nerves and anxiety. Then, when Thommo did lose his wicket, there were more than a few chairs kicked over.

It was a terrible result after fighting so long and the last person to be blamed was Thommo, who had battled enormous odds to stick around so long. I put my arm around his shoulder once we reached the rooms and told him: "Don't worry about it; you did your bit."

He was distraught and I can remember that the two of us sat staring at the floor for what seemed like an eternity. But, as they say, life goes on, even if Rod Marsh did try to lift everyone's spirits by looking under chairs, in lockers and even in cricket bags. Someone asked him what he was doing and he replied: "Looking for four missing runs."

We had a brief post mortem over a few beers that night, but we had another Test coming up and just had to get on with the job.

To make matters worse, the Poms were quaffing champagne as if it were going out of style. At the time, Thommo and I hoped they would choke on the bloody stuff as they gulped it down.

The Addams Family

Early in my Test career I was known to teammates at Pugsley and, to those not familiar with television, this nickname came from a character in *The Addams Family*; and it was none too flattering as the original Pugsley was an overweight boy with a pasty complexion.

I can blame leg-spinner teammate Jim Higgs for this sobriquet although, thankfully, not too many people still refer to me by this name - apart, that is, from Higgs himself and David Hookes.

Fortunately, I was known to my teammates and others simply as AB (my initials, of course) for the latter half of my career and this was a much more sober nickname for an Australian Test captain.

Still, here have been worse cricket nicknames! For example, how about Ian "Mad Dog" Callen, or Alan "Froggy" Thomson or David "Evil Dick" Sincock, or dare I say it in this book, Bill "Phanto" Lawry?

May blooms

Anyone who knows former Australian Test spinner Tim May would know that he is accident prone. If Chicken Little's prediction of a piece of the sky falling down came true, May would be the one to cop it on the head.

It was no surprise then when May injured a hand during the Fourth Test of the 1992-3 series against the West Indies. Fielding at the Adelaide Oval, May somehow stepped on to his own hand and gashed it quite badly. Even worse, it was his bowling hand.

We desperately needed May's spin and, after I threw him the ball and he had bowled a couple of overs, I asked him: "How's it feeling?"

"No worries," he replied. "The hand's OK and I'm doing well".

Doing well? May had a magnificent spell in which he took five overs to help us take control of the match. In fact, he was so impressed with his own bowling he told me: "This is scary AB, they're coming out so well."

To which I replied: "Well, just keep stepping on your hand."

Tony Dodemaide

A useful all-rounder, Tony Dodemaide made his first-class debut with Victoria in 1983-4 and played 10 Tests. He also played 24 one-day internationals for Australia.

Merv the swinger

Merv Hughes and I grew up playing cricket together for Melbourne District club Footscray, but he always seemed to be one step ahead of me in terms of development and, of course, he went on to become one of the best and most popular pace bowlers Australia has produced.

As everyone who has played the game knows, the craft of fast bowling must be developed through experience, as this yarn concerning Merv and his early days with the Footscray First Eleven illustrates.

Footscray at that time had a very strong attack, with Merv, Colin Miller and Len Balcam. In fact, it was so good I did not get too many chances to bowl and even Merv wasn't regarded as the main strike bowler.

In one match, I was standing at third slip and watched as Merv steamed in from his then ridiculously long run-in. I could not believe how long it took him to get to the wicket but, once there, he let a beauty rip and I was fortunate enough to take the nick.

We all rushed in to congratulate Merv, and Miller, who had been fielding at fine leg, was impressed with the late swing. He asked Merv: "What side of the ball have you been shining?"

Merv, who was a bowling rookie at that stage, was dumbfounded and could only reply: "I've been shining both sides because I want to swing it either way."

I must admit, however, that Merv was a very quick learner and served Victoria and Australia well over many years - after he learned to shine just one side of the ball.

To tell the truth

After Victoria won the 1990-1 Sheffield Shield, the team made a brief tour of England and played a match against Essex which, at that time, was the County champion. I was fortunate enough to be on that tour, along with my good mate Merv Hughes.

In fact, we batted together in that match at Chelmsford and I will never forget Merv's reaction to a loud and very confident appeal against him for a catch behind. Merv just stood and glared at the bowler, as if to tell him he had been an idiot for even thinking he had got his bat anywhere near the ball.

As it was the end of the over, I walked down the wicket and had a mid-wicket conference with him. I asked him why he had looked so annoyed.

"Annoyed?" Merv spluttered. "Wouldn't you be annoyed? If I'd just got a little more bat on that shot it would have gone for four."

Jim Higgs

A fine leg-spinner, Higgs made his first-class debut for Victoria in 1970-1. He played 22 Tests for Australia and took 66 wickets at an average of 31.16. He later was an Australian selector.

Barnacle Bill

Bill Lawry was a marvellous opening batsman, with immense powers of concentration. And, despite being dumped in favor of Ian Chappell as Australian captain late in the 1970-1 series against England, he was a cunning skipper who seemed to know how to get the best out of any situation.

For example, there was the time in 1971 when I was new to the Victorian team and Bill still had ambitions to get back into the Australian team for a 1972 tour of England. One of his main rivals was South Australian Ashley Woodcock, whose big weakness was facing spin bowling.

Initially, I wondered whether it was a coincidence that when Woodwock was batting I would be brought on for my leg-spin bowling just a few overs after the pace men had opened the bowling. If I got Ashley out, which seemed to happen regularly, I would then be taken out of the bowling attack, usually for about four hours until the last over before the tea break. This was the only time "Snorkel" seemed to use spin bowlers with any great conviction or purpose.

There also was the time we played South Australia on a terrible wicket, with the ball turning in all directions. Bill, the master batsman, saw the wickets tumble around him and, I thought at the time, must have groaned when I strode to the crease for the last wicket stand.

The wicket, a reddish clay, was a monster and SA spinners Ashley Mallett and Don Sutherland got the most from it, even if Bill managed to defy everything they tried to winkle him out.

Bill, at this time, was still nursing ambitions of going on that tour of England, and to carry the bat through an innings would have been a marvellous achievement to set before the tour selectors.

There were three hours to stumps and a Victorian win was out of the question. The best we could hope for was an honorable draw, and this was a very long shot indeed, because at that stage I had not completed the transition of my batting prowess to the high levels of later in my career.

Now, you would expect the class batsman to rotate the strike so that I would not be facing the start of each over. But not in this case - I faced the start of just about every over.

With great skill, I managed to survive for more than an hour, much to the annoyance of the South Australians. For most of this hour, Bill was at the other end of the crease, leaning on his bat.

Finally, a ball kicked off the wicket and struck me in the middle of the stomach. The South Australian shouting appealed to umpire Max O'Connell, who must have thirsty. It surely must have been the only time in cricket history an lbw decision was given against a batsman struggling to regain his breath after a blow to the solar plexus.

So Bill got his wish! He carried his bat throughout the innings. But, I am sad to report, did not make the tour of England.

Mervyn Hughes

An enormously popular Australian Test star, Mervyn Hughes generated genuine pace and was among the best fast bowlers of his era. He made his Test debut against India in 1985-6 and played 53 Tests for 212 wickets at an average of 28.83. He also played 33 one-day internationals for Australia.

Hanging around?

During a Test against Sri Lanka in Perth, I went in to bat after Australia had lost its eighth wicket. My Footscray and Victorian teammate Tony Dodemaide was about 20 not out and keen to make quite a few more runs. He walked over to me as I reached the pitch and gave me some advice.

"Just hang around," he suggested. "I've been here a while and I can get some runs from this attack."

"No worries," I replied. "I'll let you get all the runs."

I then played and missed at the first ball I faced, and ditto for the second. Then, as if in a rush of blood, I clouted the next ball to the boundary and did the same to the very next ball. "This is OK," I told myself. "I'll keep going in this vein." This was all too easy and, when the next ball arrived, I took a mighty swipe - and was bowled neck and crop.

Then, making my way back to the dressing room, I had to pass Dodemaide and he asked: "What in the hell went wrong with our plan?"

"Oh," I replied. "I just got bored."

It's not important

Cricket can generate enormous mood swings, as I discovered during the Third Test of the 1993 series in New Zealand. I was jubilant in winning one of these Tests across the Tasman, subdued when another was drawn and, well, let's not get too far ahead of ourselves.

The Third Test was played at Auckland's Eden Park and, late on the fourth day, the series was in the balance. New Zealand had five wickets in hand in its second innings, but was finding it tough going. Everyone thought this one would go right down to the wire.

The New Zealand batsmen were Ken Rutherford and Tony Blain and we desperarely needed a breakthrough to get right into the Kiwi tail. Steve Waugh was bowling when Rutherford drove a ball straight to me at knee height. "Ah," I told myself. "This is it."

I clutched at the ball but it somehow slipped through my fingers and Rutherford - and New Zealand - lived to fight another day, literally. I wished the ground would open and swallow me. I had let Australia down and was utterly inconsolable.

Rutherford and Blain saw it out to stumps and, with the Kiwis needing just 40 or so runs the following day, I knew I had blown it. There now was no way known we would win the series, and it was all my fault - or so I convinced myself.

No-one spoke to me in the dressing room and I sat brooding in the team bus on the long trip back to out hotel. I just could not get the dropped chance, and its conseqences, out of my mind.

Then, at the hotel, I was sitting in the foyer when teammate Paul Reiffel walked over to me, put a hand on my shoulder and said: "Don't worry about it. We all drop catches."

I was delighted that one of my teammates had taken the trouble to try and console me, so I replied: "Yeah, I suppose you're right. Dropped catches are part of the game."

Reiffel then floored me when he quipped: "Yeah, but none as important as that one."

To make matters worse, Rutherford and Blain got the runs the next day to give New Zealand what turned out to be a relatively easy victory.

Knowing the rules

We were playing a South Africa tour match at Pretoria when a batsman named Rule strode to the crease. Then, after Rule had faced his first ball, Tim May turned to bowler Paul Reiffel and asked: "Do you know his family?"

A puzzled Reiffel mumbled that he did not know anyone named Rule or, come to that, had met very few people in South Africa. Then, after Reiffel's next delivery ro Rule, May again asked the question: "Do you know this bloke's family?"

"I told you, I don't know anyone named Rule," Reiffel snorted.

This went on a third and fourth time and, after Reiffel's fifth delivery to Rule, May again asked the question: "Are you sure you don't know his family?"

Reiffel snapped back: "For the last time, I don't know what you're talking about. And why do you want to know?"

"Well," the laconic May drawled. "If you don't know the Rules, you shouldn't be playing the game."

Rodney Marsh

One of the greatest wicketkeepers the game has seen, Rodney Marsh made his Test debut against England in 1970-1 and cruelly was dubbed "Irongloves". Marsh made his critics eat their words by developing into a brilliant 'keeper and a punishing batsman. In fact, he was the first Australian 'keeper to score a Test century (against Pakistan in 1972-3). He played 97 Tests and claimed 355 victims (343 catches and 12 stumpings).

What celebrations?

After England had taken the Ashes Down Under in 1970-1, it was very important for Australia to jump back to a position of respect as soon as possible. The 1972 series in England therefore was critical but, by the time we came to the Fifth Test at The

Oval, England held a 2-1 series lead and already had retained the Ashes.

Victory at The Oval was vital for morale and it gladdened every Australian heart when Greg and Ian Chappell shared a 201-run second innings partnership to put us in a strong position. Ian made 118 and Greg 113 and, as luck would have it, I was at the crease when Australia was in sight of victory.

We had lost only five wickets by the time I hit the winning run after turning a ball from Tony Greig behind square leg. I danced more than ran the single and continued to celebrate in the rooms and long into the night.

It was a big, big night and I still have absolutely no idea of what time I went to bed. But who wouldn't celebrate a Test win over England, especially after levelling the series 2-2? Who said we were the worst team to tour England?

Next morning I ran into teammate Paul Sheahan, who joked that we must have drank London dry of champagne the previous night. As someone who always preferred beer and did not even like champagne, I asked: "What champagne?"

Sheahan replied: "Don't you remember? You sat next to me at dinner last night and we drank gallons of the stuff?"

What dinner? What champagne? As I said, it was quite a celebration.

Team medicine

I always feel sorry for any cricket team touring Pakistan as I know what to expect...heat, flies, poor umpiring decisions and, worst of all, little or no alcohol. As a Muslim country, Pakistan virtually is "dry", although it always is possible to get a drink if you really want one.

The only legal way to get a drink is to declare yourself an alcoholic. This entitles you to a piece of paper which, in turn, entitles you to a drink, or two or more. And, yes, a number of those on the 1982 Australian tour of Pakistan officially were alcoholics.

Even so, supplies were scarce and not up to scratch. The local beer was not a patch on Australian brews and, after a while, I dreamt each night of sitting on top of a mountain of cold tinnies, opening one after the other and slaking a raging thirst.

I finally got so sick of the lack of vital supplies that I asked staff at the Australian embassy if they could get us some good old Aussie beer. They said they would do their best for us.

Just a few days later a parcel marked "vaccinations" arrived at our hotel. There also were instructions that the contents of this parcel had to be refrigerated, for medical purposes.

And, indeed, it was the finest medicine poured down my throat.

The "medicine" was a couple of slabs of Swan Lager, one of my favorite brands from my home State of Western Australia. You beauty!

The Juggler

Yes, I readily admit to dropping three chances on my Test debut on the 1970-1 England tour of Australia. But I also took four catches and took pride in my performances, especially as the media labelled me "Irongloves". I was determined to prove them wrong and, fortunately, I was able to hold on to my spot in the Test team.

You can understand my anguish when I made what my teammates thought was a botch of a stumping chance from the bowling of Terry Jenner against Barbados during the 1973 Australian tour of the West Indies.

The truth is that Jenner spun the ball and deceived the batsman, who jumped down the wicket and swung lustily only to miss by the proverbial mile. The ball dollied to me and, with the batsman out of his crease by the same proverbial mile, I snatched at the ball.

Instead of gloving the ball, it bounced up my arm and then popped into the air. As this was going on, the batsman was walking towards the Barbados dressing rom. Finally, I lurched forward to again try to grab the ball, now on the ground, and accidentally sent the bails flying.

Ah, thought the batsman as he watched while walking, I might not be out after all. He broke into a gallop to regain his ground. Meanwhile, I again reached for the ball, only to knock two stumps out of the ground.

With the batsman just about to safely regain his ground, I made one more lunge - and this time knocked the remaining stump out of the ground with the ball in my hand. The batsman was out, but only just.

I was priding myself on finally making the stumping when teammate Greg Chappell ran in for what I thought was a congratulatory greeting. But, instead of telling me how well I had retrieved the situation, he started cracking jokes about me being a juggler.

And, tongue firmly in cheek, he told me it was one of the finest stumpings he had seen.

"Thanks," I preened myself in mock of my own effort. "But a lesser 'keeper would have made a mess of it."

Shane Warne

A national hero, Shane Warne is regarded as one of the greatest spinners to have played the game and his leg-spin wizardry has been an integral part of Australia's success over recent years. Warne made his first-class debut for Victoria in the summer of 1990-1 and made his Test debut against India the following summer. He had shoulder reconstruction surgery early in 1998.

Bang, you're dead

Despite what the cricket public might see out on the ground, Test cricketers from rival nations are not deadly enemies. Sure, we play for keeps, but I have made good friends with many of those I have played against and the memories will live with me forever.

One of my good international friends is South African all-rounder Brian McMillan, a knockabout bloke with a great sense of humor. In fact, I reckon he could almost be your archetypal, laid-back Aussie.

During one Test against South Africa, there was a knock on our dressing room door and, when it was opened, we all saw McMillan standing there with a rifle he later confessed he had borrowed from a security guard.

He had a mean scowl on his face and snarled: "I'm sick of you lot and I'm going to do something about it."

You should have seen the guys scatter but, of course, McMillan was just having one of his jokes, even if it was a bit scary at the time.

There also was the time McMillan was batting against Australia in South Africa and he took off for a couple of runs. I dared him to go for a third run, but he wasn't interested. This prompted me to suggest he was a little nervous about retaining the strike and facing yours truly in the next over.

This sparked the big South African into saying: "I'm taking you on a fishing trip and I'm going to use you as bait." He then added chillingly: "Lots of people die in South Africa, one more won't make a difference."

Jeff Thomson

A frighteningly fast bowler, Jeff Thomson terrorised batsman, especially in tandem with Dennis Lillee. Thomson made his first-class debut for NSW (he later moved to Queensland) in the summer of 1972-3 and made his Test debut in the same season. He played 51 Tests and took 200 wickets at an average of 28.01.

Your turn, partner

When I played Test cricket with my good mate Dennis Lillee, there were suggestions that we were England's twin abscesses or that we meant double trouble or, in the words popular at this time: "Ashes to ashes, dust to dust, if Lillee doesn't get you, Thommo must."

This was all very flattering, but we were just doing our job for Australia, even if it was suggested in the English media at one stage that I liked to see "blood on the wicket".

And, of course, people forget that there were times when Lillee and I bowled to each other in State matches, he for Western Australia and me (for most of my Sheffield Shield career) for Queensland.

The first time we faced each other was at the WACA in my first season of Shield cricket and, being young and keen, I did not care much for reputations. Yeah, Lillee might have been an established Test star, but I wanted to make a name for myself.

As Lillee strode to the wicket I made up my mind I would put him through the wringer but, despite my best efforts, he clipped me away for a boundary from my first delivery to him.

Enraged, I built up a huge head of steam for the next ball and let it fly as fast as I could bowl. The ball whizzed off the pitch and thudded into Lillee's gloves. I knew it had hurt him, but he tried not to show it as he scampered through for a single.

Then, when he was at my end, he looked me straight in the eye and scowled: "I just hope you can hold a %$&^* bat."

I probably was too brave for my own good when I goaded him in return: "Listen pal, you've got the bat at the moment. Just get up the other end and see how %$&^* good you are."

Darren Berry

A brilliant wicketkeeper, Darren Berry has been Victoria's number one glove-man for several years now and, in 1997, was called up to the Australian touring side in England.

Fit for a queen

I was coaching the Macclesfield club in the Cheshire League in 1997 when given the greatest thrill of my career to that stage. I was invited to join the touring Australian side after Adam Gilchrist injured a knee. Would I what!

Touring with the Australian team certainly was a tremendous thrill, but I must admit there was a time when I wished I had read more than the sports pages of newspapers or concentrated more in my history lessons at school.

That was when I was told I would be going to Buckingham Palace to meet the Queen. As I stood in the queue while team captain Mark Taylor introduced everyone, I racked by brain trying to think of something intelligent to say to her, about world events or perhaps something about the United Kingdom.

I need not have worried as everything went off smoothly and I even was able to have a chuckle when it was Ian Healy's turn to meet Her Majesty. As quick as a flash, Healy pulled out a drawing his toddler daughter had produced especially for the Queen.

Then, as we were on the team bus returning to our hotel, we all wondered whether the Queen would stick the drawing on her fridge.

Dean Jones

An enormously popular batsman, especially with Victorian fans, Dean Jones made his first-class debut in 1981-2 and played his first Test in 1983-4. He played 52 Tests for an aggregate of 3631 runs at an average of 46.5. Jones, at his peak, was considered the best one-day international cricketer of his era and played 164 limited-over matches for Australia.

Meeting the Don

I'll always remember the Fifth Test of the 1988-9 series against the West Indies, for more reasons than one. This Test, at the Adelaide Oval, provided me with one of the biggest thrills of my cricket career, and more than a few laughs along the way.

I was fortunate enough to reach 131 by stumps on the first day, only for wickets to fall early the next morning. A double century then looked out of the question when the seventh wicket fell and Tim May strode to the crease.

I need not have worried at that stage as Tim scored 24 of the next 50 before being caught by Richie Richardson off the bowling of Curtley Ambrose. We then were 8/383, with big Merv Hughes striding to the crease.

Dean Jones - congratulated by The Don

At that time, I think, Merv had a best Test score of something under double figures. As I was on 178, I considered the prospect of a double century as fairly remote. Could big Merv, never the most patient of batsmen, stick around long enough to help me towards the big milestone?

To make matters worse, I knew the Windies soon would be able to take the second new ball and their attack comprised Ambrose, Courtney Walsh, Malcolm Marshall and Patrick Patterson - a pretty handy quartet of pace men.

As soon as Merv reached the pitch he told me: "Don't worry. I'll stick around long enough for you to get your double ton. And it will cost you a beer every time I catch up with you in the years ahead."

Merv was as good as his word and, in fact, scored 72 not out while I eventually was run out for 216. Merv more than did his bit and I am still paying for it as every time he sees me he says: "Where's the beer you owe me?"

Following cricket tradition, we visited the Windies dressing room after the day's play. I took a few cans with me and Merv had an entire slab tucked under his arm. There was no way known he was going to leave early, not after bagging a personal best of 72 not out.

Then, in the rooms, he started telling everyone how he had hit Ambrose for two sixes and also had hit Walsh, Marshall and Patterson for a six each. It was like re-opening wounds, especially when he gave Viv Richards a ball-by-ball description of his innings.

Merv was probably only half-way through re-living his innings when former great West Indies bowler Wes Hall walked into the room with Sir Donald Bradman and then started introducing cricket's living legend to all the players.

Sir Donald, in his inimitable high-pitched voice told me: "Well played, Deano. Good knock." Naturally, I was more than a little pleased with myself and, looking over to Merv, I could see him preening himself for a pat on the back and a few words of praise from The Don.

But, when introduced to Merv, all Sir Donald said was: "Funny game, cricket." Merv was totally deflated and I don't know who had the bigger bottom lip, Merv or Curtly Ambrose.

Hall then introduced Sir Donald to Patterson, who had had a terrible innings with the ball and finished with the unflattering figures of 1/130 (he took the wicket of number eleven Michael Whitney).

Patterson had just been berated by Hall, Richards and Ambrose for his poor bowling performance and did not take kindly to Sir Donald's comment, which went something like this: "Geez, you bowled rubbish today, son."

I could see the whites of Patterson's eyes spinning and, as quick as a flash, he ripped off his shirt to reveal a magnificently muscled wash-board stomach and massive chest. He stood erect, making him look even taller than his imposing 194cm (6'4") and, for a split second, I genuinely feared for Sir Donald's safety.

However, Patterson merely looked down at Sir Donald and snarled: "If I bowled to you, I'd kill you, man. I'd kill you."

Sir Donald merely looked up at the giant Jamaican and said in his high-pitched voice: "You couldn't get Merv Hughes out, so how would you get me out?"

True story!

Mark Taylor

A splendid opening batsman and a superb slips fieldsman, Mark Taylor made his first-class debut for NSW in 1985-6 and made his Test debut in 1988-9. He later was appointed Australian captain to succeed Allan Border.

A familiar face

My appointment as Australian Test captain in 1994 was accompanied by a packed press conference in Sydney and, of course, my face appeared on every television channel and in every daily newspaper around the country.

As soon as I had finished the press conference I flew back to Moree where wife Judy and I had been visiting her relatives. Then, during a drive to Coff's Harbour, we stopped off at Glen Innes to see her brother and to have lunch at the local pub.

However, I could not help but notice that the publican kept staring at me and, finally, he said: "Geez, you look like Mark Taylor."

To which I replied: "Yeah, but don't you think I'm better looking?"

The publican agreed, but later twigged my real identity and apologised for his mistake. "I knew I'd seen your face," he told me and, after so much media coverage, it was quite understandable and we had a good laugh together.

Ian Healy

A superbly talented wicketkeeper and a more-than-useful batsman, Ian Healy made his debut for Queensland in 1986-7 and played his first Test in 1988-9. He holds the world record for the most Test dismissals by a wicketkeeper, breaking Rod Marsh's record of 355 dismissals during the 1998 tour of Pakistan.

G'day mate

One of the very best yarns of the 1993 tour of England concerns my good mate David Boon, who, after heeding a call of nature one night in Manchester, saw a dark-haired bloke walk up to him at the urinal.

Boon, sensing it was teammate Tim May, thought he would play a practical joke on the spinner. He therefore reached over and tickled his neighbor's private parts. The only problem was that it was not May at all, but a complete stranger.

This yarn now has reached almost mythical proportions and there even have been suggestions that after Boony apologised the stranger turned to him and said in an effeminate voice: "That's OK, big fella."

A dog of a catch

From Wayne Kell, of Beaumaris, Vic.

As captain of the Eastmoor Cricket Club in a Melbourne suburban competition, I had the usual problem of how to "hide" an
incompetent fieldsman. The poor bloke was too slow to put in
slips and too awkward to put in the deep. I eventually decided
that I would use him at short-leg to intimidate the batsmen.

My reasoning was that any chances going his way would be too
sharp for most of my other fieldsmen anyway and that I at least
would get some value from him as he was an aggressive type whose
sharp tongue would upset the opposition.

Half-way through the rival team's innings, a batsman popped
up a chance to my man at short-leg. He showed amazing reflexes

to take an extremely difficult chance very low to the ground. And, as he lay sprawled on the turf, he grinned widely as he held the ball aloft.

His teammates, myself included, rushed in to congratulate him - only to hold back at the last second. To take his wondrous catch, he had fallen straight into a freshly-laid barker's egg, which was splattered all over the front of his once-white shirt.

I kept him at short-leg for the rest of the innings - just to upset the sensibilities of the rival batsmen.

An appealling umpire

From David Green, of North Dandenong, Vic.

As a young cricketer in the mid-'60s, I played in the Oakleigh District Cricket Association with a team known as Princes Park. The club had junior and senior teams and we played all our games on matting. Our A Grade captain, Jim Sawford, was a brilliant all-rounder who could have played the game at a much higher level.

Just before the start of the 1985 season, Jim arranged a practice match against a team based in Caulfield, with both teams to have one innings each. I do not remember the scores, but I do recall a most unusual incident in the Caulfield team's innings.

It all stemmed from the fact that, being a practice match, the teams had to provide one umpire each. The Princes Park umpire during the Caulfield team's innings was our wicketkeeper, a veteran known as Clarrie.

I bowled the first over of the innings and managed to get one to swing and hit the batsman on the pads. But, before I could bellow an appeal, there was an enormously loud "'HOWZAT" from our wicketkeeper/umpire. It surely must be unique - an umpire appealling for a wicket!

The batsman, to his credit, walked without a murmur.

The star recruit

From Kevin Daniels, of Hartwell, Vic.

As captain of a struggling team in a Melbourne suburban competition, we were desperate for recruits and, in particular, for a quality batsman who could take an attack by the scruff of the neck. We had one decent batsman and wanted someone who could help him hold an innings together.

Our players cast a wide net and, imagine my surprise, when one of them came up to me at practice one Thursday night to tell me he had secured the services of a former Public School boy who was the best batsman at his school.

"He has been concentrating on university studies for the past three or four years, but has just completed his course and is ready to have another crack at cricket," my teammate informed me with enormous enthusiasm.

I hardly slept on the Friday wondering whether the star recruit would bother to turn up to play in our minor competition. After all, from what I had heard of his prowess he should have been wielding the willow with one of Melbourne's District clubs.

I need not have worried as the star recruit turned up well before the start of play and, to my instant joy, looked every centimetre an athlete. On the old scale, he was about six feet (182cm) and there did not appear to be a gram of fat on his lean, lithe body. I licked my lips in anticipation of our team at last being able to compete with the better sides in the competition.

After winning the toss and electing to bat, I listed the star recruit at number three. Where else? After all, this was our batting saviour, the man who could make light of the pie-throwers in this little suburban competition.

As usual, we lost an early wicket. It was time for the star recruit to show his wares and, as he strode to the wicket in immaculate whites and a brand new pair of batting gloves, my soul soared.

The bowler, of course, had no idea our hopes rested with this new batsmen, but tore in nevertheless. He sent down what he thought was a delivery at least as fast as Dennis Lillee could bowl but, in reality, was no more than a slowish-medium which did absolutely nothing off the pitch or in the air.

However, it was accurate. And, with the star recruit taking a mighty hoik, the ball cannoned into the stumps. It was, to say the least, the shot of a man who had never played cricket at any decent level.

I could hardly contain myself and, as the star recruit started removing his pads, I asked: "I thought you were the top batsman of your Public School year?"

"I never said that," he replied. "I said I had gone to Public School and that I once had been the top batsman at school."

It transpired that the star recruit indeed had gone to Public School, but his great batting exploits had been at a country State school with an enrolment of 14 - 11 of them girls.

No-balled

From Ken Crawford, of Enfield, NSW

Years ago, when playing junior cricket in suburban Sydney, both teams were in a dither over how to start the game. We had tossed the coin, with my skipper electing to bat, but there was one major problem. There was no ball.

We emptied cricket bags, looked in lockers and even scouted the long grass surrounding the oval...to no avail. Finally, someone had the bright idea of looking in the boot of his father's car. Lo and behold, we found a cricket ball - more brown than red and with the stitching coming apart. But it was a ball and the game could go ahead.

The match was about an hour old when our worst fears were realised. One of our batsmen took a mighty swipe at a loose delivery and the ball sailed over the boundary and, indeed, over a private railing fence.

We all knew this meant trouble as the owner of the property was cantankerous at best and often had complained about us hitting cricket balls into his beloved flower beds. We peeped over his fence with considerable anxiety, worried that we might have broken stems from a rose bush and crushed a planting of petunias.

Finally, after what seemed an eternity, we finally were convinced that no-one was home and that we were free to jump the fence and search the back garden for our one and only cricket ball.

It took just one minute! There it was, in the deep end of the swimming pool. And, just as one of our intrepid cricketers was stripping to his jocks to retrieve it, a door opened. It was the cantankerous property owner.

"What in the %$^* hell do you think you're doing?" he bellowed.

None of us could even mumble a reply and, in fact, it took us less than five seconds to sprint to the fence and clear it. My mate in the jocks was the first to clear the fence and, with his whites under his arm, had to make a dash for the dressing room.

As far as I know, the ball is still at the bottom of the pool. And, by the way, the match was declared a draw.

GETTING EVEN

From George Moore, of East Brunswick, Vic.

During a match between Box Hill and Brunswick in the Victorian Sub-District competition some years ago, Brunswick batsman Alan Walton was given out lbw and was far from happy with the decision.

Then, in the next innings, he was clean bowled. But, instead of walking, he straightened the stumps, put the bails back in their groove and got ready for the next delivery - much to the Box Hill team's dismay.

One of the umpires finally told Walton that he most definitely was out. To which Walton replied: "After the other decision I thought you might like to even things up."

WRONG-LEGGED

From R.M. Callender, of Queenstown, Tas.

Here are several true tales from my time in cricket:

A chap was playing a cricket match for the first time and, when he finally had his turn to bat, marched out to the wicket with just one batting pad - on the wrong leg. When told of his mistake, he simply replied: "Don't worry. I'll go up the other end."

Also, in a match involving Tasmanian team Gormonston, a batsman broke a sandshoe on the tough gravel ground (with concrete wicket) and called to his team's twelfth man to bring him a new shoe. Then when the twelfth man asked him which one, the batsman replied: "The right-hand foot."

Finally, in a Country Week match many years ago, a batsman hit the ball for a six into a strawberry patch and started running. But, as time was all-important in this match, one of the fieldsmen said to a teammate who had found the ball: "If you pick it up, I'll stand on your bloody hand."

Praying for rain

From Alan Gleeson, of Parkville, Vic.

I was playing in a mid-week match in bayside Melbourne in 1982 at the height of a heatwave in which the temperature soared to more than 40 degrees Celsius. Conditions, to say the least, were stifling and, to make matters worse, my team was facing almost certain defeat.

There were more than two hours to stumps and we had just four wickets remaining and no hope of scoring the 150-plus runs for victory. It was a case of dig in to salvage a draw - except that we knew in our hearts that the remaining batsmen were bunnies. It looked a forlorn task.

However, a glimpse to the south gave us great encouragement

as the sky was an ominous black in the distance. In fact, it looked like a cracker of a thunderstorm brewing along the edges of Port Phillip Bay.

A wicket fell, but we all looked to the sky. The storm was closer. Another wicket fell, and we all looked to the sky. The storm was almost upon us. A strong northerly wind blustered and blistered us and, with just two wickets remaining, we prayed for the heavens to open.

And they did! But, instead of rain, top soil was dumped on us from a great height. The sky's blackness had not been caused by storm clouds, but by soil and other matter in the atmosphere whipped up during one of the worst droughts to hit Melbourne.

The dust storm passed within minutes, leaving everyone choking and in even more need of a shower. Even worse, the sun again shone brilliantly and we lost our last two wickets within minutes. It did not rain again in Melbourne for another month.

Caught, by C. Gull

From Colin Fisher, of South Oakleigh, Vic.

I know this tale might be hard to swallow as there are countless stories of animals and birds being involved in unusual cricket occurrences and even dismissals. However, I swear this is a true story, even if it occurred only in a social match at a suburban Melbourne park one Sunday afternoon.

As the match involved drinkers from two Melbourne hotels (in the early '90s) the rules were, to say the least, relaxed more than a little. One of the game's rules stipulated that a batsmen be given a "life" if dismissed first ball. Little did we know we would be invoking that rule very early in the match.

The match was less than half an hour old when the third wicket fell and a new batsman strode to the crease. He took block and, as he already had consumed several cans of beer, was in a hurry to get back to his drinking. He just wanted to swat the ball as hard as he could.

The bowler trundled in and the batsman belted the ball fair and square in the middle of the bat, straight into a slow-moving and careless seagull flying about three metres overhead.

It was an extraordinary hit in itself but, as the gull dropped dead to the ground, the ball also was diverted straight into the hands of a fieldsman. The final decision? Not out! After all, the incoming batsman had to be given a "life" after being "dismissed" first ball. And a "life" was more than could be given the poor seagull!

This surely must be the only time in any cricket match in which a batting stroke killed a bird in mid-air, a fieldsman caught the ball before it hit the ground and the batsman was given not out.

I am convinced that if it had happened in a Test there would have been a report on the front pages of newspapers the next day.

Stumped, by a dog

From Arthur Collins, of Thomastown, Vic.

We all have heard of dogs wandering on to a cricket ground and interrupting play. However, one particular dog went a little too far when it scampered to the pitch during a game in Melbourne's northern suburbs a few years ago.

I was fielding at slip when I first spotted the big black dog, nose to the ground as it meandered over the oval. With unerring accuracy, it made its way to the wicket area and eventually did what all male dogs do to woodwork - had a pee on the stumps at the bowler's end.

We all laughed, with one exception. The umpire at that end was mortified and called in his colleague from the square leg position. They had a brief discussion and, although I strained my ears to hear their conversation, I could not make out a word.

LEG BEFORE WICKET!

The game continued and, in the next over, one of the batsmen was bowled. The stumps flew through the air and the fieldsmen, myself included, danced jubilantly. Just seconds later, the umpire at the bowler's end marched down the wicket to re-arrange the stumps.

This was most unusual as, in most cases, the umpire at square leg would put the stamps back in position. As the bails were being balanced in their grooves, I asked the attending umpire why he had come down the wicket to do the job.

He replied: "My colleague has a phobia about dogs and, after what happened to the stumps, insisted he would not touch them again."

Although one of my mates washed the stumps during the luncheon break, the fussy umpire still refused to touch them. And, in a way, I could hardly blame him.

The last innings

From Clive Powell, of Deniliquin, NSW

Although I played rugby at a fairly high level during my youth, cricket always has been my passion. I played my first game when I was about six years of age and represented the one Sydney suburban club for more than 30 years, mainly as a batsman who could turn his (right) hand to a bit of off-spin bowling.

When I shifted to northern Victoria in my early 50s, I thought I had played my last game of cricket. However, the local cricket club was short of players and I agreed to make up the numbers for the thirds. I did this for five years and, at 59 years of age, finally retired.

We shifted again and, well retired, I contented myself with watching my new local team in action - until the day I was told they were three men short and asked to help them out - just for this one match.

I had just celebrated my 60th birthday and, along with a couple of other old fogies, agreed to don the creams yet again. I had put on a bit of weight after retiring a couple of years earlier and was worried sick about how I would manage if we had to field all day in the hot sun.

It was a scorcher of a day - no wonder several of the younger blokes had cried off for the afternoon - and, thankfully, our skipper won the loss and elected to bat. I sincerely hoped I would not have to field until the following Saturday.

This was wishful thinking as our first five wickets fell in the first 40 minutes. I groaned at the prospect of a total collapse and then spending the hottest part of the day chasing leather.

Another wicket fell and then another. As only the old blokes were left to bat, it looked as if we would struggle to make it to mid-afternoon. Then another wicket and another. We were nine down for about 50 and it was my turn to bat. I hadn't held a bat for several years and, to say the least, my technique was rusty.

Still, I could only do my best and, after reaching the middle, my batting partner - the team captain - walked over to me and suggested I let him have most of the strike. I wholeheartedly agreed, especially as I was convinced I would not last more than one or two deliveries.

The skipper worked his plan to a treat by smacking the odd boundary and then pushing for a single towards or at the end of each over. I managed to survive the few balls I faced and the score mounted from 9/50 or so to about 9/75. It was easily the best partnership of the innings.

There was only one problem. Every time the skipper called for a quick single, I had to take off like a jack-rabbit. He might have been able to make his crease without too much trouble, but I had to pound down the wicket like a demented sumo wrestler.

The opposition soon twigged on to the fact that I was probably the slowest runner between wickets in the history of the game and targetted me every time. And, every time, I just managed to reach the safety of the crease.

To everyone's surprise, the score mounted. We had batted for more than an hour and I was exhausted. The skipper was about 40 not out and I had made just the one run. However, my legs felt like lead and my poor back ached as if it would snap in two.

There was only one thing to do - hit out or get out. I told the skipper I had had enough and he agreed with my plan. I therefore played every agricultural shot NOT in the cricket textbooks. I hoiked and hoiked and hoiked until I had reached close to 60. Not bad for an old bloke!

Unfortunately, I hoiked once too often - and too short. I had been smashing the ball to the boundary, but this time I had to run, and run and run. I was convinced there were three runs in the shot and, with my belly bouncing as I made my way back for the third run, I heard the crash of timber and joyous shouting.

I turned around to see the umpire's finger in the air. The skipper had been run out. And, as he wheezed to me as we left the ground, he admitted to sheer exhaustion. It made my day and, even better, I convinced myself there was life in the old dog yet.

The skipper and I had pushed the total to 147 and our team had to field only for an hour or so late that afternoon. We bundled the opposition out cheaply the next Saturday - a much cooler day - and I celebrated with my new teammates at the local pub.

My hoiking heroics convinced me to keep playing but, unfortunately, I failed to reach double figures again that season and I immediately retired, again - for good. Unless...

The spoils of war

From Bert Musgrove, of Henly Beach South, SA

As a Briton who migrated to Australia in 1949, it is only natural that I still follow England's Test fortunes. However, I have the utmost respect for Australian cricket, especially as I learned very early just how tough the Aussies play the game.

I served in the British Army in north Africa during World War II and my mates and I played cricket or soccer whenever and wherever we could. Our biggest problem was finding the right equipment. As you can imagine, there were not too many shiny red cricket balls in or around Tobruk.

We therefore had to "make do" and our favorite trick was to fashion pieces of rubber from the tyres of bomb-wrecked lorries and other military transport. Our pitches often consisted of hardened sand.

The games, to say the least, were rough and ready and the usual pleasantries of cricket were ignored. We played to win, especially when we arranged scrub "Test" matches against Aussie soldiers.

During one game, an English batsman took a mighty swipe at the ball and hit it into scrub surrounding our "ground" - a cleared patch. An Aussie chased after the ball and, after flicking through the scrub for what seemed an eternity, finally made a return.

When the 'keeper finally gloved the ball he looked at it in amazement. It was not the dark roll of rubber we had been belting around for the past hour or so, but a genuine cricket ball, with only some of the shine missing.

What on earth was a cricket ball doing in the middle of the north African war zone? We all moved in to handle and stare at the mysterious cricket ball. Obviously, we made the most of our good fortune by completing the match with our great new discovery.

It was only weeks later that I learned that a team of British officers had played a scratch match against a team of non-commissioned officers at the very same clearing we had used. And one of the officers had brought the cricket ball with him from England.

What were the odds of another cricket match being played at that scrubby patch of ground and what odds that our home-made ball would roll into the very same area where the genuine cricket ball had been lost?

Double whammy!

From Bruce Smedley, of Prahran, Vic.

I still shudder at how I was dismissed in a junior (Under 16s) match in a south-east Melbourne competition about a decade ago. To make matters worse, I was on 48 and almost certain to reach my half-ton when dismissed in most unusual circumstances.

The bowler was a straight up and down plodder and there were plenty of runs for the taking. In fact, I had smacked two consecutive balls to the boundary before again trying to hit him down the ground.

The ball stopped on me a fraction and I mis-timed it so that it flew back down the wicket about half a metre from the ground. Unfortunately, my batting partner did not have enough time to get out of the way and, as he turned his back to allow the ball to pass, it hit the edge of his bat and flew higher into the air.

It was the simplest of chances and the bowler gobbled it up with glee. I was out caught and bowled when, with a little more luck, I would have posted my half century.

OWZAT? WHATZAT?

From Greg Moody, of Corowa, NSW

When I was playing junior cricket in the Murray Valley Cricket Association I discovered that one of the umpires was as deaf as a post and, as you can imagine, this made it extremely difficult for him to tell whether or not a ball had been nicked for a catch.

He invariably gave the batsman the benefit of the doubt, unless the ball deviated quite obviously. You have no idea of how many batsmen made big scores, yet now would admit they should have been given out several times.

In one incident the batsman hit the ball and was caught behind. The deaf umpire merely stood there and asked the batsman: "Did you hit it?" I seem to recall the batsman had a wry smile on his face as he shook his head in the negative.

In another incident, the fielding team went up as one for an lbw decision to scream "'owzat?" The deaf umpire merely looked at his wrist-watch and answered "three o'clock".

The cream of cricket

From Mark Patterson, of Trafalgar, Vic.

City folk have absolutely no understanding of life in the country and of the sacrifices we have to make, even when it comes to the simple joys of life - like a social game of cricket.

My tale stems from a football grand final in Gippsland, with my team being pipped on the final siren. We were devastated and, at our wake that night, decided we would make amends the following season. And, as we drank more and more, someone came up with the idea of challenging our conquerors to a game of cricket so that we would not have to wait a full year for revenge.

The next morning, someone somehow managed to remember that idea and the challenge was made, and met. Arrangements were made to play at a neutral venue just before Christmas. If we couldn't beat them on the football field, we would beat them at cricket.

The big day dawned bright and sunny. In fact, it was bloody hot, with not a cloud in the sky. Rain certainly would not interrupt this grudge match and we looked forward to taking revenge.

We won the toss and sent the opposition in to bat under the 50-overs per team rule. Play started early, at 10.30am, to give us plenty of time to complete the match, and competition was ferocious from the very start.

Our rivals smashed every loose delivery and our bowlers threw themselves into their work. We took a few wickets, but they made more than a few runs. By the time the 50 overs had been completed our rivals had scored 8/227 - a sizeable target, but acheivable.

We started well, scoring 30 runs off the first four overs. However, we then lost a couple of quick wickets and the incoming batsmen got bogged down. Even worse, the early north wind gave way to a sticky stillness. A storm was in the brewing.

It now was a race against the weather. There was no way we were going to settle for a draw and our batsmen threw caution to the wind, with considerable success. After 35 overs, we were 4/138 and in a strong position - if only the rain would hold off.

Then, in the 42nd over and with just 38 runs to score, and with five wickets in hand, lightning ripped the sky and the rain bucketed down. The thunderstorm lasted more than an hour and, when it passed, the outfield was soggy.

As we were playing on a concrete wicket, we knew we had to wait only an hour or so for the outfield to dry for the resumption of play. However, our rivals did everything in their power to prevent a resumption.

They complained about tiny pools of water deep in the outfield and, at one stage, even suggested that there was about to be another thunderstorm. Finally, however, we resumed play - at about 6pm.

The bowlers dawdled through their overs and, still with five wickets intact and just 20 or so runs needed for victory, the match came to an abrupt halt when one of the bowlers rolled around in agony after being hit on the shin from a shot down the ground.

I strongly suspected he was not hurt at all, but there was little anyone could do about it. His mates fussed over him and finally decided he would have to be carried from the ground. All this took more than 10 minutes and, at just after 6.30pm, our batsmen called it quits.

As one of them explained: "We all have cows to milk."

To make matters worse, our rivals thrashed us at football in both our clashes the following season.

Caught, by the master

From John Miller, of Burnley, Vic.

As a young cricket fan I was fortunate enough to go to a school (St Patrick's, East Melbourne) not far from the MCG. It was common for a group of us to walk through the Fitzroy Gardens to the MCG at the end of lessons. This invariably enabled us to see the last session of play.

Early in the 1959 school year there was speculation that Australian pace bowler Ray Lindwall would break Clarrie Grimmett's record of 216 Test wickets for Australia. It was the Fifth Test of the series against England and, not wishing to miss a bit of cricket history, a mate and I "wagged it" from school during our lunch break.

Later that afternoon we saw Lindwall get his record and, no sooner had we sat down after the great man had been given a standing ovation, than there was a hand on my shoulder and a voice whispered in my ear, "Good afternoon, boys".

It was our form master and, as you can imagine, our blood ran cold. However, we need not have worried as he then said: "I thought I'd find you here. I'm a bit of a cricket fan myself and didn't want to miss the record."

We watched the cricket together for more than half an hour before he pulled his punchline: "I knew you two had wagged it, but did you know that I gave the rest of the class the afternoon off in case they also wanted to get down here?"

We had taken an almighty risk for nothing, but thank goodness our master had a sense of humor - and was a cricket fan. And Lindwall got the record!

Wilde about cricket

From Peter O'Brien, of Greensborough, Vic.

What do you do when your school insists you go to a play and you are desperate not to miss a ball of a Test being played in England? The obvious answer is to plug in to a transistor radio.

This is what I did during a performance of Oscar Wilde's "The Importance of Being Earnest", a play we were studying for English Literature as part of our matriculation year of 1961. However, the Ashes were far, far more important and word was passed to my schoolmates, from row to row, with every run made by Australia.

Unfortunately, however, two wickets also fell (to Freddie Trueman, if my memory serves me right). Although some sections of the audience were able to laugh along with the actors, our little group remained decidedly glum.

Finally, it was all too much when we lost our third wicket of the day I could not help myself exclaiming loudly : "Bloody hell!" The words echoed around the theatre and, for a second or two, the actors lost the plot.

I shrivelled in my seat as I waited for the eventual arrival of one of the masters. I fully expected a tap on the shoulder, but not the violent tug on the ear that eventually heralded his arrival. I was marched out the theatre and told to go home and report to the principal the next day.

I went through mental agony that night and, next day, copped the physical agony when I was given six of the best from the principal's leather strap. The funny thing is that I wrote an essay on Wilde for my examination later that year, and did well.

A fighting innings

From Richard Moody, of Corowa, NSW

One of the best-loved sports characters in the Murray Valley area about 20 years ago was a bloke known to all and sundry simply as Teddy, an accomplished sportsman who had had 208 professional fights as a middleweight and even had a bout with Australian champion George Barnes.

Teddy could turn his hand to any sport - cricket, football, tennis - and do well. Yet, for all his ability, he was severely handicapped in middle-age when he injured an eye in a mill accident.

When batting, Teddy struggled until he learned to shut one eye to eliminate the blur from his injured eye. And, of course, he had to give football away. Instead, he turned to goal umpiring, for his local team.

In one cricket match Teddy scampered down the wicket when called for a quick single, only to be at least two metres short when the return hit the stumps. Then, as the umpire had his finger half-raised, Teddy turned to him, put his clenched right hand to his left bicep and gave him the "up yours" signal - along with the comment: "You'll get it up to there if you give me out."

I have never seen an umpire react so quickly. The finger went down and I distinctly recall the words "not out" being spoken in a quivering voice. After all, the umpire knew only too well of Teddy's fighting abilities.

In another cricket incident, Teddy removed a wicket and threatened to spear the umpire after being given out in a controversial lbw decision.

And, although this is a cricket book, it is worth telling of the time Teddy made a bodgy decision as a goal umpire. Although a shot went straight through the middle, Teddy - umpiring for his team, literally - put up one finger for a behind.

The full-forward who had kicked the goal ran over to Teddy and called him a "******* cheat". Teddy replied with his fists and knocked the full-forward out cold. Naturally, there was a huge rumpus and the umpire ordered everyone from the field in an attempt to regain control.

Officials from the two clubs met to discuss the situation and it was decided that Teddy could not continue as goal umpire. But who would be brave enough to tell him? The task was left to Teddy's club president.

However, he took every precaution by locking himself in the club rooms and calling Teddy from an open window. Then, after giving Teddy the bad news, slammed the window shut for his own safety.

Sadly, Teddy died a few years ago, but his legend lives on in the Murray Valley.

HOWZAT!

Also from Richard Moody, a cricket poem:

The bowler leapt into the air,
The 'keeper's arms spread wide,
The slips all yelled and turned to stare,
Mid-off hugged point just like a bear.
All thought the umpire wise and fair, so left him to decide.

The man at bat seemed unperturbed.
He shuffled round the crease.
The loud appeals had not been curbed,
The leg-side bail HAD been disturbed,
But the ump's dread word was still unverbed.
The batsman's tried to look at peace.

The ump looked set with his decision.
The batsman bent and said:
"I'll put this bail back in position,
Today's strong wind could blur one's vision."
The ump replied with great derision:

"Yes, hold your hat as you go out, lest it blow off your head."

A double blow

From Tony Greenberg, of Ormond, Vic.

It was the opening game of the season and, in my excitement the previous week, I bought a complete new cricket outfit - shirt, trousers, sweater, boots - the whole kit and kaboodle.

I was playing for East Brighton Thirds and watched as the wickets tumbled on a very lively wicket in a one-dayer. Then, with the score at 9/50 it was my turn to bat. In all honesty, if I had to bat higher than 11 my team would be in real trouble in every match. So that gives you some indication of my batting ability.

I wish I could have told the bowler at the other end of my batting record as he was swooshing the ball all over at the place, at some considerable speed for this little suburban competition.

His first delivery to me was a bouncer and, being a bunny, I tried to hop out of the way. No luck! The ball smacked me fair in the gob and there was blood everywhere. Funnily, my first thought was not for my gashed mouth, but for my brand new cricket clothes. Oh no, I thought, not blood on my shirt and trousers!

But there was worse. As I lay sprawled on the ground, a rival fieldsman came running in to help me - and stepped on my glasses, which had fallen off in trying to get out of the way of the bouncer.

My mouth healed, the clothes washed out, but I had to buy myself a new pair of glasses.

Hard to impress

From Jim Arthur, of Thornbury, Vic.

I was batting in a social match about 10 years ago and, not being a regular cricketer, wanted to make an impression for my nine-year-old son, who had just taken up the game with a local club.

Now this might have been a social game, but it was between the local football club and its cricket counterpart and the standard was quite high. Indeed, the match was played on a turf wicket and one of the opposition bowlers had played at Sub-District level the previous season.

I batted at fifth wicket down and was determined to show my son I knew a thing or two about cricket. There was no way known I was going to be dismissed cheaply and my concentration was total.

The bowling was tight and accurate and, at times, frightening for a bloke who had not played on a regular basis for the previous seven or eight years. Balls whistled down outside my off-stump and the spin from the former sub-district player teased and tormented me.

But I stuck to my task and refused to be tempted into rash strokes. I played within my limitations and helped my team to a respectable total while several wickets fell at the other end.

Then, when I finally was dismissed after more than 90 minutes at the crease - to a doubtful lbw decision, I might add - I was more than a little pleased with myself. I had scored just eight runs, but had held up my end while my partners had gone about the task of smashing boundaries.

As I reached the dressing room I patted my son on the head, fully expecting him to sing my praises. Instead, he told me: "Geez, you were boring, Dad." Thanks son!

...And these will bowl you over

Jingle balls

The great W.G. Grace was so confident of his batting ability he refused to bat with a box...until late in his career when confronted by Surrey speedster Tom Richardson, renowned for his ability to bruise and even break bones.

After one joust with Richardson, Grace declared it was time to protect the family jewels and therefore decided to have one specially designed for him.

The only problem was that the good doctor asked an eccentric engineer named Croome to come up with the right design, and the final product was elaborate - to say the least. In fact, every time a ball thudded into the box there was a loud metallic clang which eventually drove Grace to distraction.

He finally lost patience and walked from the ground to confront the box's inventor. "I told you to make me a box, not a music box," he snarled at Croome.

G-lovely way to go

Derbyshire batsman Alan Revill, a top County batsman just after World War II, came up with a novel means of dismissal when he shook his hand after it was hit by a bouncer. Revill's glove fell on to the wicket and dislodged the bails.

Lost in the bush

The excitement built with every over in a match between Monbulk and Knox, in Melbourne's outer eastern suburbs. Knox made 9/205 one Saturday, with the home team batting well to reach 4/188 with 10 minutes to stumps the following Saturday. The situation looked grim for Knox, which could only play for a respectable draw over the final overs.

Even worse for Knox, a Monbulk batsman smacked a boundary off the first ball of what should have been the third last over. The ball skidded over long grass and into a patch of bush. The bowler, disconsolate at the prospect of defeat, walked back to the start of his run.

Turning, he noticed that the other members of his team had disappeared from view. He walked to where the ball had last been seen and, coming to a clearing, saw his 10 teammates sitting and smoking.

"Can't find the ball?" the bowler asked.

"Yeah, I found it, but who wants to give it back?" the captain replied.

The delaying tactic looked like working until the Monbulk players woke up to the ruse and insisted on returning to the field for one more over. A Monbulk batsman smacked a six into the bush off the last ball of the match for victory. No-one bothered looking for the ball!

Out, but not out

England opening batsman Andy Lloyd has the rare distinction of having gone through his entire Test career without being dismissed. In the First Test against the West Indies in 1984 he scored 10 before being hit on the head by a ball from Malcolm Marshall. He spent the next five days in hospital and was never again selected to play for England.

Absent - in jail

Cricketers have missed Test matches through illness, injury and even to attend a relative's funeral. However, England's Edward Pooley is the only man to have been unavailable for selection because he was in jail. Pooley, a wicketkeeper well-known for his betting habits, discovered a novel means of gambling in New Zealand.

He bet a Canterbury identity one pound to a shilling that he could nominate every member of the local team to make a duck the following day. The bet was accepted and Pooley then surprised the local by suggesting EVERY Canterbury player would make a duck.

The ruse was obvious: Pooley would have to fork out a shilling for each batsman to score, but would collect a pound for every duck. Pooley should have pocketed sizeable winnings, but got himself into a fight with the local and was carted off to jail. A charge of assault was dismissed but by the time Pooley arrived in Australia it was too late. And he never played Test cricket.

Jockey or the horse

C.B. (Charles) Fry probably was the greatest sports all-rounder the world has seen. He not only played cricket AND soccer for England, but also was a world record holder in the high jump and excelled at many other sports.

C.B. Fry -
great all-rounder

On retirement from active sport, he told a friend he was thinking of taking up horseracing. The friend replied: "What as - horse, jockey or trainer?"

Fry, who also was a noted academic, was in charge of the Royal Navy training ship Mercury, at Hamble, Hampshire, just after World War II and retained his love or cricket by coaching the cadets.

However, age respects no-one and when Fry could not repeat the strokes of his golden youth, sometimes resorted to language more commonly heard below decks. Indeed, he fired a full volley of abuse when he once stood on a stray ball and fell when bowling in the nets.

Bright spark

There was a rest day during the India-England Test at Bombay in 1980 because of a total eclipse of the sun. Ian Botham took 13 wickets and scored 114 in England's 10-wicket win. With typical Fleet Street humor, one English newspaper headline read: "Botham Brightens England".

Breaking the ice

England Test hero David Gower had a lucky escape when a car he was driving in St Moritz, Switzerland, in 1990 crashed through ice and sank. Gower walked away unhurt.

At the double

A bowler named Roberts took a "double hat-trick" - six wickets with six balls - in a match between Victorian country sides Tatura and Mooroopna in 1935.

The *Tatura Free Press* of January 22, 1935, reported the story under the headline "Roberts' Six Wickets With Six Balls":

"The match between Tatura and Mooroopna was begun at Tatura on Saturday. Mooroopna batted first and Maskell and Powell bowled to Foley and Thorne. With the score at six, Powell bowled Thorne for a duck. When the score stood at 1/15 Roberts relieved Maskell. Foley and Helmer, batting well, hurried the score on and Bartlett relieved Powell.

"Roberts struck form with the ball and secured two wickets in his next over. His figures read 2/11.

"Nine came from the next over from Bartlett, before the sensation of the match occurred. Roberts took the remaining six wickets with six balls. This feat is unique, and it certainly is a record for the Shepparton Association. His bowling figures read: eight wickets for 11 runs off 23 balls. The Mooroopna total was 41."

The Mooroopna scoreboard read:

A. Foley,	lbw Roberts		15
H. Thorne,	b Powell		0
N. Helmer,	b Roberts		14
A. Noonan,	st Binns	b Roberts	1
P. McCarthy,	not out		9
R. Dennis,	b Roberts		0
J. Furze,	b Roberts		0
R. Morton,	b Roberts		0
A. Green,	lbw Roberts		0
G. Baker,	b Roberts		0
K. Maher,	absent		0
		Extras	2
		Total	41

Bowling: Maskell 0/9; Powell 1/19; Roberts 8/11; Bartlett 0/10

Bradman misses

The great Don Bradman was encouraged to apply for the position of Melbourne Cricket Club secretary just before World War II. After giving the matter considerable thought, Bradman made an application, but was overlooked in favor of former Australian batsman Vernon Ransford (20 Tests from 1907-8).

A bad trot

Australian Albert Trott, who made his Test debut against England in 1894-5, took his cricket talents to England and qualified to play with Middlesex before playing two Tests for England against South Africa in 1898-9. Middlesex gave him the privilege of a testimonial match against Somerset, only for Trott to bowl so well that the match finished early.

This deprived him of considerable income and he grumbled: "I have bowled myself into the work house." Tragically, Trott's poverty caused him to shoot himself on July 30, 1914.

A showcase shot

The great Walter Hammond, batting for England in a match against the Dominions in 1945, hit a six through the Long Room's open door at Lord's. The ball bounced into a glass showcase but, fortunately, there was no damage.

Fore...

Dr W.G. Grace is credited with the introduction of four runs for boundaries, first mentioned in the Laws of Cricket in 1884. However, there were no boundaries when Dr Grace first played at Lord's in 1864 and he wrote: "If the ball struck the pavilion a four was allowed, although even that rule was suspended for one year, while every other hit had to be run out."

Dr Grace then advocated the introduction of four runs for boundary hits after a player chased a ball into the crowd and an elderly spectator, "not being sufficiently alert to get out of the way", was seriously injured.

All in a day's play

County club Warwickshire suffered the indignity of being dismissed twice by Surrey in the one afternoon in 1953. To make matters worse, Surrey defeated Warwickshire by an innings and 49 runs - all on the afternoon of May 16. Warwickshire was dismissed for 45 within 75 minutes in its first innings, with Surrey then making 146.

Warwickshire then made just 52 in 70 minutes in its second innings. Surrey's Tony Lock took a hat trick in the first innings and not one Warwickshire batsman was bowled in either innings.

But there's more... Lock was being hit on the head while batting for Surrey and then rushed to hospital. The English media described it as the most extraodinary day's play in any English County championship match.

Wisden Women

Isabell Duncan made cricket history late in 1998 when she became the first woman to feature on the front cover of Wisden Cricket Monthly. She was one of 12 women cricketers interviewed in the lead-up to the vote by Marylebone Cricket Club members on whether to admit women to the 211-year-old club.

The MCC in September 1998, finally voted in favor of women joining the club, but only after considerable controversy and after it had been pointed out that, otherwise, it would be ineligible for funds from the British Government.

All for nothing

Opening batsman Jock Sutherland carried his bat for Wakatu in a match against Nelson during the 1977-8 New Zealand season. Nothing extraordinary about that, except that Sutherland did not score in his team's meagre total of 21.

Bunny makes good

Australian pace bowler Bill Johnston was not noted for his batting and, in fact, had a highest Test score of 29 and a highest first-class score of 39. Yet he returned from the 1953 tour of the West Indies with an average of 102: he was dismissed just once.

You're blind, ump!

Australian batsman Sid Barnes was noted for his dry sense of humor and, in one match during the 1948 tour of England, went out of his way to make a point to an umpire who dismissed an appeal. He picked a dog which had wandered onto the field, took it to the umpire and said: "All you need now is a white stick."

ETON V HARROW

Cricket matches between English public schools Eton and Harrow, first played in 1861, pre-date even the English County Championship (1873), Test matches (1877) and the first Lord's Test (1884).

These mataches attracted huge attendances at the turn of the century, with more than 38,000 attending the two day's play between Eton and Harrow in 1914 and newspapers even carried special reports until recent years.

One of the most famous matches was in 1910 and forever will be known as "Fowler's Match". Harrow scored 232 and, after dismissing Eton for just 67, seemed assured of victory - especially when Eton was 5/65 in its second innings.

Harrow, however, had not counted on the fighting spirit of Eton's Fowler, who held the tail together for a second innings total of 219. Although Harrow needed just 55 runs for victory, Fowler took 8/23 to give Eton a win by nine runs.

Fowler's deeds made headlines and a telegram simply addressed to "Fowler's Mother, London", was successfully delivered.

What a spectacle!

The bewhiskered C. Aubrey Smith not only won critical acclaim as a Hollywood actor late in life, but also played Test cricket for England at the turn of the century. The autocratic-looking Smith, who played Robert Taylor's uncle and colonel of the regiment in *Waterloo Bridge* and starred in many other top movies, helped form the Hollywood Cricket Club and delighted in entertaining many of the world's leading cricketers.

In one match against an Australian side comprising the great Don Bradman in 1932, the elderly Smith fielded at slip. However, his reflexes much slower than when in his prime, Smith muffed a relatively easy chance. He looked at his hands to see if there were holes in his palm and, finally deciding that there was nothing wrong, signalled for his butler to attend him.

Smith relayed a message and play was held up while the butler raced off to get Smith's spectacles. But, minutes later, Smith dropped another sitter. This time he removed his spectacles, examined them intently and snorted: "Good God, the man has brought me my reading glasses."

I beseech thee...

English batsman the Rev. David Sheppard incurred the wrath of teammate Fred Trueman during a Test against Australia in the summer of 1962-3 by dropping several chances. Trueman eventually turned to Sheppard and fumed: "You might keep your eyes shut while praying, but when you're fielding to my bowling, you keep your eyes open."

Yankees just dandy

Australia once lost a match to a team from the American city of Philadelphia during a brief tour of the United States in 1893. In fact, the Aussies went down by an innings and 68 runs, with the local side amassing 525 in its first innings. The tourists could manage only 199 and 238.

Monkey antics

Excitement was high in the match between the venerable Marylebone Cricket Club and New South Wales at the SCG on February 8, 1879. The MCC, led by Lord Harris, appeared to gain the upper hand when it successfully appealed for a run out decision against Billy Murdoch, Australia's finest batsman at that time.

NSW captain Dave Gregory was so incensed he walked from the pavilion and remonstrated with umpire George Coulthard, an Englishman. Gregory then took his men from the field when Coulthard refused to change his mind over the run out decision.

Fans invaded the ground, with one spectator striking Lord Harris with a cane. The MCC's Albert Hornby immediately raced to his captain's rescue and grabbed the cane-weilding thug by the scruff of the neck and marched him to the pavilion and into the arms of waiting police officers.

It was no mean feat by Hornby, nicknamed "Monkey" because he stood just 5ft 2in and had the reputation of scurrying around the field "like a monkey after a peanut".

In one match for The Gentlemen against The Players at The Oval, "Monkey" Hornby was brilliantly caught high in the deep by giant (6ft 4in) fieldsman Willian Gunn. "Monkey" was not

Lord Harris - struck by a cane

impressed and, on his way back to the pavilion, snapped at Gunn: "My luck to be caught by a giraffe."

Praise the lord!

The Honorable Francis Stanley Jackson undoubtedly was one of the great cricket identities of the Edwardian era. Educated at Harrow and captain of Cambridge, he was an excellent all-rounder whose cricketing ability and leadership qualities made him a natural to captain England.

In addition, he became a member of parliament, president of the Marylebone Cricket Club and even Governor of Bengal. Recalling Jackson's funeral in 1947, the Bishop of Knaresborough once said: "As I gazed down on the rapt faces of that vast congregation, I could see how they revered him, how they revered him as though he were the Almighty, though, of course, infinitely stronger on the leg-side."

The best laid plans...

England was cock-a-hoop when it gained a 2-0 lead in the 1936-7 Ashes series. England, sensing a series victory, therefore attempted to tighten the noose for the Third Test and England captain "Gubby" Allen even came up with a plan to dismiss the great Don Bradman. He told fieldsman Walter Robins that, when given the signal, he had to run from square leg to long leg in the hope that Bradman would hook.

The plan worked perfectly, with Bradman hooking and Robins running to exactly the right position - only to drop the chance. The remorseful Robins apologised profusely, only for Allen to reply: "Don't give it a thought, Walter. It has probably cost us the rubber, but don't give it a thought." Bradman made 270 and Australia won by 365 runs. Australia went on to win the series 3-2.

A drink to victory

The Times, in a report in 1840, told of a most unusual match, between the Teetotalers and the Whiskey Drinkers. The report read: "The Temperance men mustered strong and were backed by Lord Clancarthy and Admiral Trench.

"After a well contested game, the patrons of the mountain dew won by the match by 35 and celebrated their victory in the evening by illuminating their houses, bonfires, etc, much to the discomfiture of the Mathewites, who fought a hard battle."

SNAP HAPPY

Frank Laver was a great all-rounder who not only was Australian player-manager on the 1909 tour of England, but was an expert photographer who took many shots of his teammates during lighter moments on tour.

For example, Laver took this photograph of champion Australian batsman Victor Trumper in a cart being pulled by goats. And his uncomplimentary caption read: "Ready For a Drive - A Fine Pair".

He also took this 1905 photograph of Australian cricketers pigeon shooting at the Whanganui River, New Zealand, en route to England.

Better late than never

The great Dr W.G. Grace was a ferocious competitor, as evidenced by an incident in the final over of the day in one match. Dr Grace was fielding when the ball thudded into the batsman's pads. There was no appeal but, during the evening, the batsman confessed to Dr Grace that he thought he would have been given out lbw if there had been appeal.

Then, before the first ball the next morning, Dr Grace stood at the wicket and shouted: "'Owzat!" The umpire then gave the batsman out, lbw from the last ball of the previous day.

It has been suggested that Dr Grace was a law unto himself when it came to whether or not he had been dismissed. In one match a bowler twice was left utterly dejected when Dr Grace refused to walk after apparently snicking the ball to the 'keeper.

Then, when the bowler eventually removed the great man's leg and off stump, he snorted to Dr Grace: "What are you waiting for? The middle stump as well?"

Dr Grace did not exactly endear himself to Australian fans and, during the 1891-2 tour by England, there were several complaints of "bad sportsmanship" and even downright rudeness to his hosts.

One of the complaints centred around Dr Grace's attitude when Australian Robert McLeod had to leave the field during the Second Test after learning that his brother had died. When the uncompromising Dr Grace was told that the replacement was a much better fieldsman, he insisted on an alternative substitution.

On the same tour, Dr Grace was reported to have complained about the state of wickets and the size of grounds and once refused to allow Australia's Jack Blackham to use his lucky coin for a toss.

Dr W.G. Grace - a law unto himself

But, to shed light on the other side of Dr Grace's character, there is the yarn about him visiting a country town on one Australian tour and, when the hosts told him there was no water for bathing, he replied: "What do you think I am; a water spaniel?"

On another occasion Dr Grace was bowled first ball and refused to budge from the crease. In fact, he insisted it had been a "trial" ball. When the bowler protested, Dr Grace replied: "The fans didn't come here to see you bowl. They came here to see me bat."

Three for...

This tale probably is not true but is one of the best yarns concerning cricket catches and originated with Queensland medium-pace Bill Tallon, whose brother Don kept wickets for Australia. Bill Tallon was bowling for Queensland at the Gabba when he got a ball to move off the seam for a catch to brother Don. "One for none," was the way Tallon told the yarn.

He continued the story by telling how he got the ball to swing again for another wicket, again caught behind by brother Don. "Two for none," Tallon would exclaim in telling the story. However, the fall of the second wicket brought the great Don Bradman to the crease.

"Not to worry," Bill Tallon thought, as this day he was able to make the ball dart around and, when he dropped one short, Bradman went for the hook. Brother Don got under the ball and took the catch. "Bloody beauty," Bill exclaimed. "Three for 284!"

Cases of dropsy

Writing of catches, there have been a number of extraordinarily inept fieldsmen to have played Test cricket and even the great Dr W.G. Grace, a bulky man at the height of his fame, was loathe to move too far from the wicket and dropped more chances in slips that he would have cared to remember.

Then, of course there were the countless chances missed by Les "Chuck" Fleetwood-Smith, the Australian left-arm spinner. Fleetwood-Smith had to be "hidden" in the field because of his notoriously poor concentration. He had a reputation for making bird calls from the deep - even when he was turning to bowl - and drove teammates to distraction by shouting "Come on, Port Melbourne" whenever the mood took him.

Fleetwood-Smith's fielding and catching was on a par with another Australian Test cricketer in Bert "Dainty" Ironmonger, who at least had an excuse - he had lost a finger in a chaff-cutting accident.

Ironmonger, who worked as a garbage-collecter, was asked late in life why he had never been selected to tour England and replied: "I guess it's because of the noise I make when I eat soup."

Bowling a myth

During the West Indies' first tour of Australia in 1930-1 it was decided to take in a movie the night before the start of play in a match against Victoria at the MCG. The touring party took particular note of a cinema advertisement for a brand of cricket bat used by Australian and Victorian batsman Bill Woodfull, who was described in the advertisement as "unbowlable".

Learie Constantine immediately declared that he would prove the advertising material incorrect - and was as good as his word. He bowled Woodfull for a duck the next day.

Cricket krauts!

Cricket has been played in almost every part of the world, from Siberia to Timbuktu. It has been played on almost every conceivable surface, from ice to sand. But did you know that there once was an unofficial "Test" match between England and - wait for it - Germany? The series resulted from an invitation to the Leicestershire County Cricket Club to play a series of matches against several German teams, including a "Test" against a combination from the Berlin Cricket League, in 1911.

The Leicester team sailed for Hamburg and made its way from there by train to Berlin. The first match was against the Union Club - on matting on a football pitch. Leicester made sauerkraut of its opponents and then defeated a team known as Preussens before facing the combined Berlin side.

Again, the result was a formality and it even was noted that the German wicketkeepers adopted the unsual style of taking the ball on one knee.

The Leicester mail reported: "On every hand it is said that our visit has done German cricket a world of good and they are highly satisfied with the cricket given by the Leicester club."

Then, in 1937, the Gentleman of Worcestershire visited Berlin for a three-match tour. The July 31, 1937, edition of *The Cricketer* reported: "The visit of the Worcester players should do much good, especially as Herr Hitler has shown an interest in cricket."

The Germans, to say the least, were out of their depth and thrash-ed in each match. In fact, a 52-year-old English tourist made 140 in one match before exhaustion got the better of him. It was reported that after being dismissed he fell asleep, without removing his pads, in a deck chair. The century-hitting batsman later was presented with a swastika pin as a trophy.

Expecting decisions

An expectant mother umpired a match in the Central Gippsland Cricket Association competition in 1978. Mrs Lynn Crawford was seven months pregnant when she took to the field wearing dark slacks, a floral maternity shirt and floppy white hat.

Use your helmet!

Australia was playing England at Old Trafford, Manchester, in 1948 when Lindsay Hassett dropped two chances in the deep off Ray Lindwall's bowling. Lindwall, despite his frustration, at least showed a sense of humor when he removed a policeman's helmet and offered it to his teammate for any possible third chance.

In the soup!

It has been suggested that England pace bowler Les Jackson played just the two Test matches because his table manners were inferior to his cricketing ability. It has been reported that Jackson, a rough and ready customer, just started tucking into a bowl of soup at a swish cricket function when he commented: "'Eh waiter, the cook forget to warm the soup." It was a Continental-style cold soup.

All in a day's work

Australian batsman Charles Macartney was in a mood for runs against Nottinghamshire in 1921. He smashed 345 in one day - a feast of big hitting at first-class level. However, there have been even more frantic batting efforts at the lower levels of the game.

For example, Greg Beecroft scored 268 runs in just 92 minutes for Yass Wallaroos against Williamsdale at Canberra in 1979. Beecroft smashed 29 sixes and 11 boundaries.

You'll keep!

The 1890 Australian team to England contained a wicketkeeper who had never stood behind the stumps. Tasmania's Kenny Burn was a batsman who did not even get to keep wickets to relieve regular 'keeper Jack Blackham on tour. Yet every other member of the touring part had a turn as 'keeper.

Burn's selection was one of the greatest cock-ups in the history of the game and was the result of inter-colonial rivalries. With Blackham, the automatic first choice as 'keeper, the tourists needed a back-up and Victoria put Jack Harry's name forward. New South Wales responded by nominating Sid Deane.

Finally, Blackham commented to a selector that he had heard that Burn had been 'keeping very well in Tasmania. The only problem was that Blackham had mistaken East Hobart batsman Kenny Burn for Hobart 'keeper James Burn. The truth was not discovered until the team was on the boat for England.

Kenny Burn played just two Test matches for Australia, but only as a batsman. He had a meagre average of 10.25 from four innings, with a top score of 19. He died in 1956, at 91 years of age.

Bound to be tired

A 19-year-old playing in the Dandenong and District Cricket Association joined the likes of Don Bradman and Bill Ponsford when he scored a quadruple century in 1994. Corey Hojnacki smashed 426 runs, including 36 boundaries and an amazing 31

Jack Blackham - an honest mistake

sixes. He said after his mammoth innings: "I am a bit tired now; I wish I had hit more fours and sixes so I didn't have to run so much."

Horsing around!

A match between the Gentlemen of the Dale and the Gentlemen of the Hill in England in 1794 was probably one of the most unusual cricket contests of all time as it was played on horseback!

Sons of a gun

The Maharajah of Patiala was one of India's great cricket patrons between the wars and could have sired an entire competition of cricketers, as his harem produced 98 sons. There is an apocryphal tale that several visiting cricket stars once wandered past a large group of children playing in a yard. The visitors asked if this was a school and were shocked when the local guide reported that it was the Maharajah's family home.

Hop to it, Hoppy

The great "western" movie star William Boyd - Hopalong Cassidy to his adoring fans - once played cricket for the Hollywood Cricket Club. Short of numbers for a match, Cassidy volunteered his services in the belief that cricket was "a simple game". It has been reported that when Cassidy strode to the crease at number nine, he told the bowler: "Start pitching". Then, when he connected with the ball, he took off for a home run.

Just ducky!

A Northamptonshire batsman named Wilson had the unhappy distinction of being run out twice without facing a ball in the same match, against a touring New Zealand side, in 1931. To make matters worse, this was Wilson's one and only first-class match as he was never again selected for Northamptonshire.

A cricket dope

Sri Lankan customs officers became suspicous when they examined the luggage of a German tourist in 1986 and discovered half a dozen cricket balls. What was a German doing with cricket balls?

Police eventually sliced the balls open and discovered a hidden cache of drugs.

What a waste!

Yorkshire fast bowler Emmott Robinson was a typical product of his cricket-loving County; he was the salt of the earth. As a professional cricketer, he was both determined and ruthless. However, he also had a great sense of humor, as one famous incident in a match against Cambridge University in 1924 illustrates.

Robinson, after taking a wicket, turned to the pavilion to glare at the incoming batsman. The Yorkshireman could not believe his eyes as a dandified young student strode across the turf.

The batsman was Arthur Gilligan, who later was to captain England. He was wearing brand new pads, the whitest of shirts, a spanking new Cambridge cap and immaculate silk batting gloves.

Gilligan twice politely asked the umpire for "two legs" and, after twice marking his crease, turned to face the enraged Robinson. Gilligan's infinite care in taking block was a monumental waste of time as Robinson's first ball scattered the stumps.

Walking back to the pavilion, Gilligan turned to Robinson and commented: "Well bowled."

Robinson, without batting an eyelid, replied: "Aye, but were wasted on thee."

A rising star

Ian Craig created cricket history when he made his Test debut for Australia at 17 years and 239 days, the nation's youngest Test star. This debut was against South Africa in the summer of 1952-3, soon after smashing a double century for NSW against the tourists.

Craig's father claimed at his birth that "a new Bradman had been born" but, sadly, Ian contracted hepatitis and although he captained Australia, he never quite lived up to expectations.

However, when Craig toured England with the 1953 Australian team, the English were terrified that Australia really had discovered a new Bradman and, during one famous cricket dinner, one speaker commented on the baby-faced 17-year-old: "Every mother in England will pray for him, at his going in and his coming out."

Muscovite ducks

A cricket club was established in Moscow in 1993 - a century after Tsar Nicholas II laid a cricket pitch in the grounds of the Imperial Palace at Peterhof. Indeed, the British in the late 19th century saw cricket as a potential benefit for Russia, as this report from British Consul General George Stanley to the Home Office in 1881 would indicate:

"Not only among the peasantry, but among the educated classes a more healthy and manly tone of feeling is required.

"The Governor-General, Prince Dondoukoff-Korsakoff, on seeing the English play at cricket, remarked to me that could he but introduce it among the Russians, it would go far to put a stop to Nihilism; but he despaired of being able to do so, adding that when a Russian lad arrived at 15 (years of age) the only way he knew of proving his manliness was to be seen walking with some notorious person of the other sex.

"Later, with minds and bodies enfeebled by early excesses, they became easy tools of designing persons, who, under the specious pleas of philanthropy, appeal to the false sentiment engendered in them by their manner of life.

"He was speaking of civilians, especially those of the student class. The duties imposed on those who entered military schools led to a more healthy tone of feeling."

If only the British had their way, there still might be a tsar of Russia!

A testing time

New South Wales batsman Keith Rigg did not know whether to celebrate or despair when he received a telegram from the Australian Cricket Board of Control early in 1931 to tell him he had been selected to represent Australia in the Fifth Test against the West Indies. Rigg's dilemma stemmed from the fact that, at the time he was required for Test duties, he was scheduled to sit for a university examination.

Rigg wrote to the University of Melbourne Arts faculty for permission to miss the examination and, instead, sit for a "supp" - a later supplementary examination. The university gave its formal approval and Rigg travelled to Adelaide for the big match - only for Australia to name him twelfth man.

The police explode

Cricket administrator Ray Steele was manager of the 1972 Australian team in England when he was involved in one of cricket's more embarrassing practical jokes.

The Australian team had stopped at a roadside café when the team physiotherapist decided to have a joke at Steele's expense.

When Steele placed his heavy briefcase on a counter, the physio told one of the waitresses: "He's got a bomb in his bag."

Unfortunately, the passing comment hit a nerve as there had been a wave of IRA explosions in England around that time. The waitress immediately called the police and, within minutes, armored vehicles had raced to the café.

Steele settled the problem by opening his brief case to reveal its innocent contents and then handed the police team autographs.

A mean machine!

It was during the controversial 1998 England-South Africa Test series that a British inventor announced he had designed a machine to eliminate the doubt over lbw decisions. The inventor declared emphatically that his machine could determine precisely whether the ball would have hit the stumps.

Of course, there was immediate derision and scorn. British newspaper columnist Quentin Letts, in *The Daily Telegraph*, wrote:

"Each wicket, just like each dropped catch, and each honeyed off-drive, can teach us something about life. In my last term at prep school, a time of my life when many a 13-year-old stands in danger of becoming a shade too pleased with himself, I was dismissed lbw after scoring a very feeble three runs in an important match.

"I persuaded myself that the ball had pitched outside leg. On my way past the umpire I offered him my spectacles, suggesting, with over-elaborate politeness, that they might save him from repeating such a transparent error.

"The headmaster, watching from the boundary, screamed my name, summoned me and rightly gave me an almighty rocket for such impertinence. 'You will never ever again argue with an umpire,' he said. I have not done so since. But were a machine to repeat such a decision, I could not promise to avoid laying into the thing with bat and boot until it fuses blew."

A student of form

India, hit by injuries and poor form during the 1959 tour of England, called up a 20-year-old batsman studying at Oxford University. Abbas Ali Baig responded to his country's call by making 112 in his Test debut.

Grassed!

Two cricketers playing in the Heidelberg Cricket Association (Victoria) took 17 runs off one delivery for Banyule in a match against Macleod in 1990. Gary Chapman pulled a delivery to midwicket and took off immediately. Chapman and partner Chris Veal ran the 17 when the ball disappeared into long grass. It was a fortunate hit as Banyule won by just one run.

The wild colonial boys

Cricket has been one of Australia's most popular sports almost from the time Botany Bay was settled in 1788. Early Governor Lachlan Macquarie once ordered convicts to chop trees to make cricket bats for his son.

Betting was rife in early matches played in the colony of New South Wales and this often led to violence. Here, for example, is a contemporary report of a match played between the Victoria Club and the Military on January 1, 1844:

"It was then about three o'clock and the players adjourned to take some refreshment. While the game was suspended, some constables arrested a few drunken men who had been causing annoyance. A crowd of blackguards, however, rushed the escort and liberated the prisoners.

"Stones were thrown and a general row began. The mounted police were sent for but before they arrived things had quietened a little and the match was resumed. The Victoria Club made a splendid start in the second innings, the first three wickets putting on 120 runs.

"The crowd then became restless again, and as it was found impossible to keep the ground clear, the match was adjourned. One man was seriously injured through being tripped while running across the ground. The cessation of play was the signal for further unrest, and something in the nature of a riot took place, but order eventually was restored by the police."

Tit for tat

England fast bowler Fred Trueman was cutting a swathe through an amateur team in Yorkshire when a middle-aged batsman in garish club cap and brand new gloves strode to the wicket. The batsman earlier had made the mistake of urging his own pace bowler to attack Trueman, who subsequently was dismissed cheaply.

The middle-aged batsman now was quaking in his boots and suggested to Trueman that because it was a scratch match with little or nothing hingeing on the result, the England bowler should give him one ball as a "sighter".

Trueman nodded his agreement and then thundered: "Aye, and with the next ball I'll pin you to the bloody sightscreen."

Blind as a bat

Sam Loxton, batting for Victoria in partnership with the great Neil Harvey in a match at the MCG, asked his teammate: "What's my score?" Loxton was not prepared for the answer: "Don't ask me. Let's wait until lunchtime so I can get closer to the scoreboard." Harvey might have been one of the most brilliant batsmen of the post-war era, but he was notoriously short-sighted.

A genuine all-rounder

New Zealand wicketkeeper Frank Mooney was a man of many parts. In a Test against South Africa in 1954 he not only kept wicket, but opened the batting and bowled a maiden over.

Cop this!

Legendary Victorian Football League identity Jack Dyer served in the Victoria Police with another brilliant footballer in Laurie Nash, who also played Test cricket for Australia. The two sports heroes played cricket together for the Victoria Police against their NSW counterparts before World War II, with Nash terrifying the New South Welshmen with his fast bowling.

The faster Nash bowled, the more Dyer urged him to speed up his deliveries - only for one brave NSW police officer to snick the Test man through slips for two consecutive boundaries. The enraged Nash then snorted: "A bit of bodyline will fix you up". He then signalled for Dyer to stand at short leg.

The NSW batsman fended off the next head-high delivery and then copped one in the arm. "That's just for starters," Nash fumed. "The next one will get you." And it did! Nash bowled him.

Hit out, or else!

This yarn is probably not true but does reflect the need for all cricketers to think through a game. A slow and stodgy batsman named Quaife was playing for Warwickshire against Hampshire, with quick runs the order of the day. In fact, the Warwicks captain gave Quaife specific instructions: "Hit out, or else."

Quaife obviously was a creature of habit and took his time in the pursuit of runs. Finally, at the fall of a wicket at the other end, the Warwicks captain instructed the new batsman: "Run Quaife out and get the runs."

The new bastman did as he was told by calling for an impossible run. Quaife took off, only to see the ball delivered into the wicketkeeper's gloves. Quiafe was out of his crease by half the length of the pitch.

However, the Hampshire wicketkeeper was awake to the Warwickshire ploy and, instead of breaking the bails, tossed the ball back to the bowler. Quaife safely made his ground, but eventually got the message - and the runs.

Bowled, but not out

There are no specific records to indicate whether this is a true story or not, but there was a report in a Melbourne newspaper in 1992 that a batsman was bowled but given not out because the bail flew into the air and landed back in its groove on top of the stumps.

There also was a report in 1987 that this also happened to Australian batsman Michael Haysman when he was playing for a rebel Eleven against the South African President's Eleven. However, the circumstances were slightly different.

Haysman had scampered down the wicket for a quick single, only to be caught short of his ground by a direct hit on the stumps. The bails flew into the air and fell back into their grooves.

It figures...

The great Dr W.G. Grace drove scorers crazy (there were no scoreboards at that time) in one of his final matches. He kept asking about his score and, with half an hour to stumps and just short of a century, he surprisingly declared his team's innings closed.

Dr Grace's puzzled batting partner asked him to explain and the great man replied: "I have made many centuries and some ducks, but I'm told the only score I have not made between the two is 93, so when I reached that figure I declared."

Oucho, gaucho

A Marylebone Cricket Club team toured South America in 1926 at the invitation of the Argentine Cricket Association. It was the first time the MCC had made an international tour without a single game against a team from the British Empire.

The tour, to say the least, was extraordinary. The first match of the tour was played in Uruguay, followed by visits to Peru and Argentina. The MCC played 10 matches on tour and, believe it or not, went down to an Argentine team by 29 runs in one match.

The PM's a mug

When Bob Hawke - later Prime Minister Hawke - was a student at Oxford University in 1954 he was invited to play for the university against the Marylebone Cricket Club at Lord's. Although Hawke was named twelfth man, he took his duties very seriously and even asked his captain, Colin Cowdrey, about the quirks of fielding at Lord's.

Cowdrey, later to captain England, told the future Australian prime minister that as the Lord's ground had a slope, it was vital to get right down to the ball.

GET A BAG!
YER MUG!

To Hawke's great delight, he eventually was called onto the field. Then, when Raman Subba Row (later to play for England) smacked a ball in his direction, he forgot his captain's instructions.

The ball flew between Hawke's leg and a fan yelled out: "Get a bag, yer mug." And, as Hawke recalled many years later, this derogatory comment was made with a cut-glass English accent. Ouch!

Dog-gone!

Play was stopped during the final day's play in the 1962 Third Test between England and Pakistan when a dog wandered onto the pitch. All attempts to nab the culprit proved futile and he eventually wandered off the ground unescorted.

L-plate cricketers

The West Indies had a unique motto on their first tour of England, in 1906. It was: "We have come to learn, sah!" And learn they did, sir!

How to beat the Don

It was during an Australian tour match against one of the English Counties in 1934 that one bright spark came up with an idea of how to see Don Bradman off early. A spectator yelled out: "Give him 300 and ask him to go out."

Out, and off!

Victoria and New South Wales always have been bitter cricket rivals. Indeed, the very first match played between the colonies, at the MCG in 1856, almost was abandoned because of a squabble over which team would bat first.

Then, in 1863, the Victorian team went within a whisker of forfeiting a match in Sydney after a series of mishaps. Firstly, the ship carrying the Victorians to Sydney ran into foul weather and was delayed for more than 24 hours. This forced the match to be postponed.

The Victorians then were upset by a run out decision by the NSW umpire and left the field in protest. Sydney fans, in retaliation, threw insults and stones at the unpopular Victorians. This was all too much for two of the Victoran cricketers, who immediately walked away from the match. NSW defeated the nine-man Victorian team by 84 runs.

In a class of his own

An Essex wicketkeeper named Risk was sick and tired of the sight of the great Don Bradman hitting boundaries past cover point in a match at Southend in 1948 and eventually asked The Don: "Can't you hit them anywhere else?"

Bradman did not say a word in reply, but pulled the next three balls to the mid-wicket boundary before turning to Risk and quipping: "How's that?"

Not so fuzzy

A Fijian team - known at the time as the Fuzzy-wuzzies, toured Australia in 1907-8 and won five of its 26 matches. The Fijian captain was a member of the royal family, Prince Ratu Penaia Kadavulevu.

The Fijians were enormously popular and were known to the Australian cricket public by their nicknames: King Billy, Tit Willow, Flibbertigibbit, Punch, Jack Lyons, Ping-Pong, Friday, Bunny, The Wild Man, Wee McGregor and, most unflattering of all, Cockroach.

Team members would oil themselves before play and then take the field in grass skirts and head feathers and one contemporary report said: "Prior to commencing play they gathered in the field and chanted, and their song was greeted with hearty laudits."

The Australasian carried this report: "The captain of the team is Prince Ratu Levu (an abbreviated version of his name), the hereditary prince of Fiji and a grandson of the late King Thakambau. The prince is an extraordinary batsman and an all-round cricketer of more than ordinary merit.

"The second in command is Prince Rate Pope (pronounced poepay), the nephew of Prince Kadavu. Epile Seniloli is a blood relation of Prince Kadavu, and next in line of succession to the extinct kingship. He is about 23 years old, has a striking appearance, as was educated at the Suva Public School. He speaks, reads and writes English perfectly.

"Ratu Rabonu stands 6ft (182cm) high and is a good right-hand medium change bowler. Toroca is the head of the native police at Bau and is a good all-round cricketer. He is also a champion swimmer.

"Samu Bainivanua is the best runner in Fiji and is a fast right-hand (though not an express) bowler. Kikan Manasa is one of the official cup-bearers to Prince Kadavu in the great ceremony of nagona drinking. Bele is the town policeman of Bau, and a good change wicket-keeper.

"Esala is very smart in the field and also performs well with the bat. Ta Kikeikata, the baby of the team is only 17 years old, but is a promising all-round cicketer, and a smart bowler. Meleti Raimuria is a petty chief in Fiji and non-commissioned officer in the Bau constabulary."

Unfortunately, the Fijian cricketer known as "Cockroach" is not identified.

The great Coghlan?

Great Australian batsman Victor Trumper was born in New Zealand as the illegitimate son of a housemaid. One of his mother's cousins agreed to raise the boy in Australia and his name was changed from Victor Coghlan.

A huge blooper

Revered English broadcaster Brian Johnston was asked to make the public announcements at the end of the 1993 Ashes series and was given a list of the guests who would be appearing on the balcony.

Colleague Jonathon Agnew grabbed the list and made one small alteration. Johnston duly read down the list and eventually announced that officials welcomed the managing director of the sponsor insurance company, a Mr Hugh Jarse!

Never too late

Victorian pace bowler Harry Alexander made a huge mistake in underestimating the NSW attack on Boxing day in 1931. With Victoria set to resume its first innings with class opening batsmen Bill Woodfull and Bill Ponsford at the crease, Alexander decided there was no need to hurry to the MCG.

Years later, he took up the story: "The weather was fine, the wicket was good, we had a strong line-up and I batted last. I believed it would be quite safe to come into the game about lunch-time.

"I caught the train to Flinders Street Station and then hopped on a tram outside Young and Jackson's Hotel to take me to the ground. When I got on, someone said, in passing, that Victoria already were out and had batted one short. I nearly fell off the flaming tram!

"Apparently the ninth wicket had fallen with about eight minutes to go before lunch. Woodfull said it was lucky it hadn't been a few minutes earlier or I would have been missing when I was supposed to open the bowling."

The Bradman controversy

The cricket world could hardly wait for the resumption of Ashes matches following World War II and all eyes were on the great Don Bradman in the First Test at Brisbane in 1946. Would he be as good as he was before the war?

Bradman settled over his bat and, when on 28, appeared to edge a ball from Bill Voce to Jack Ikin at second slip. Ikin held the "chance" and the Englishmen fully expected Bradman to walk.

Then, when the great man remained at the crease, they appealed. Umpire George Borwick rejected the appeal and England captain Walter Hammond mumbled: "A fine...way to start a series."

In Bradman's defence, he always insisted the ball had hit the ground off the bottom of his bat before going to Ikin in slips. Bradman went on to make 187 and Australia won by an innings and 332 runs.

The big promotion

Sri Lankan medium-pacer Kosala Kuruppuarachchi decided to broaden his cricket experience in 1985-6 by playing Melbourne Dictrict cricket with the Ringwood club. Unfortunately, however, he had a lean time of it and eventually was dropped to the Ringwood Third Eleven. Just months later he took 5/44 on his Test debut for Sri Lanka against Pakistan in Colombo.

Falling on deaf ears

Australian captain Lindsay Hassett gave wicketkeeper Don Tallon, padded up to bat, this advice late on day one in a Test on the 1953 tour of England. "When you go out there, give the lights a go." Hassett, of course, was referring to an appeal against the light.

A wicket fell and Tallon strode to the crease with his captain's advice ringing in his ears. But, instead of playing cautiously and asking the umpires about the light, he thrashed at every ball.

He survived to stumps, but the unhappy Hassett demanded:"Why didn't you follow instructions and give the light a go?"

The dumbfounded Tallon replied: "I thought you said 'when you get out there, have a go'." Tallon's nickname was "Deafy".

Hassett, who was well-known for his sense of humor, was an extremely popular identity on the 1953 tour and, after hitting one century, was surrounded by admirers wanting his autograph. He had borrowed a bat from teammate Arthur Morris for his innings and, when he returned to the pavilion, there was no bat in sight.

Morris queried this and when he complained to the Australian captain that it was his favorite bat, Hassett replied: "Ah, but you should have seen the look on the boy's face when I gave him the bat."

A fast exchange

Australian batsman Greg Chappell, facing New South Wales' Len Pascoe in a Sheffield Shield match in Sydney, hooked a ball off his toes for a risky boundary. The ball flew through the air, with Pascoe screaming "Catch it!".

Then, when the ball thudded into the fence, Pascoe turned to Chappell and fumed: "I thought you could hook?"

Chappel, not to be intimidated, replied: "And I thought you could bowl fast."

The exchange infuriated Pascoe who stormed in for his next delivery determined to wipe the smile from Chappell's face. In his excitement, he overstepped the mark. However, the ball whistled dangerously close to Chappell's nose and Pascoe, after following through, snorted: "Fast enough?"

"Yes", Chappell replied. "But can you do it from 22 yards?"

Hijacked!

The Australian team to England in 1972 stopped in San Franciso - and almost into a political storm. Victorian batsman Paul Sheahan had taken ill during the flight and retired to a toilet. He fell asleep and did not return to his seat on landing. A security guard discovered a locked toilet door, smashed it open and was convinced Sheahan was a potential hijacker.

The "garden hose"

Pakistani all-rounder Imran Khan sprayed so many deliveries early in his career that he was nicknamed "Garden Hose". It also has been suggested that when he ran in to bowl the umpire would tell the batsman: "Right arm over, anywhere!"

Smile for the camera

When Australian pace bowler Ian Meckiff was called for throwing in a Test against South Africa in December 1963, there was national outrage. In fact, one cricket nut even threatened to shoot umpire Col Egar.

However, Australian wicketkeeper Wally Grout was able to turn the grim situation into a joke. When settling behind the stumps, he asked Egar to move sideways. The puzzled Egar asked: "What's all this about?"

Grout shouted back: "There's a bloke right behind you in the stand holding a camera. He's got a gun inside it. If he misses you, he'll get me."

Me, too!

The Australian team, sick and tired of being pelted by objects thrown by fans, staged a walk-off during a one-day match against Pakistan at Karachi in 1982. Pakistan's Imran Khan turned to Australian captain Kim Hughes and said: "I don't blame you going off. They throw things at me here, too."

All gummed up

Australian all-rounder Ken Mackay was noted for his habit of chewing gum and, when touring England in 1961, was inundated with gum sent by fans.

Mackay recalled: "It seemed every cricket fan in England wanted to give me gum. I had every brand and color imaginable. If England had run short of the stuff in 1961 I could have supplied every gum-chewing Briton for a month. But my prize gift was a gum-belt, fully loaded. One throughful admirer had made it and posted it to me.

"It consisted of a strip of leather with loops for sliding over a belt and fitted with small holsters similar to those on a cartridge belt. In each holster was a pack of gum. Wearing my belt I looked like the original Western gunman, with gum on the hip for a lightning draw."

No right is wrong

Australian pace bowler Geoff Lawson was so nervous in preparing to bat in a one-day match at Edgbaston in 1981 that he wore two left batting gloves. He did not realise his mistake until he was almost at the crease and, deciding that it would be too embarrassing to return to the pavilion, batted in some discomfort. He made 33 not out.

A boost of confidence

The tension was almost visible when Australian number 11 Lindsay Kline went in to bat against the West Indies in the Fourth Test of the exciting 1960-1 series. Kline and Ken "Slasher" Mackay were the only two between an honorable draw and defeat.

Kline, knowing that he had to survive for almost two hours to save the Test, had a nets session in preparation and confessed later that spinners Johnnie Martin and Norman O'Neill had bowled him a dozen times in just 20 minutes.

At one stage a woman standing behind the nets did everything she could to shatter Kline's confidence by telling him: "We can't rely on you, can we?"

Kline told her: "No, I'll have to do a bit better, won't I? But if I get rid of all my 'outs' now, perhaps I won't have them when I get out in the centre." Of course, Kline did survive with Mackay for a famous draw.

Out, one way or the other

An Australian team was playing the South Zone team at Bangalore during a tour of India in 1969 when wicketkeeper Ray Jordon queried an umpire after being dismissed for a duck. The umpire replied: "Mr Jordon, if you hit it, you were out caught. If you say you did not hit it, you were out lbw anyway."

This did not deter the next man in, John Gleeson, who said to the umpire: "See that pad. If the ball hits that pad and you put your finger up, this bat will be wrapped around your head." Gleeson is reported to have survived a dozen lbw appeals in making 18 not out.

Spider bite

Dashing Australian batsman Doug Walters, knowing that teammate Ashley Mallett had a dread of spiders, decided to play a trick on the spinner by putting a fake spider in his pocket before he was due to field.

Walters then waited for the perfect moment and, when Mallett was called on to bowl, removed the toy spider from his pocket, stuck it on a piece of chewing gum and attached the lot on the ball. When Mallett saw the "spider" he threw the ball faster than Dennis Lillee could bowl it.

Not for quids!

When batsman Ian Redpath debuted for Australia in the 1963-4 series against South Africa he played as an amateur so that he could continue playing football with the Geelong team in the Victorian Amateur Football Association.

He explained later: "At that time of my life, sport was very important to me. Not just cricket, but all sport. I felt it would be stupid to jeopardise my status prematurely simply for the sake of an extra few pounds."

Have a spell

During an England-Australia Test at Old Trafford, Australian captain Richie Benaud gave the ball to Queenslander Tom Vievers and told him: "Just have this over while I change the bowlers around."

Vievers did much more than that. In fact, he bowled 51 overs unchanged in just over five hours of play. At one stage he strode past Benaud and quipped: "Pretty long over, isn't it, skipper?"

Benaud explained later: "Tom's first over was so good - he could have had Ken Barrington first ball - that I couldn't take him off."

Dutch treat

Believe it or not, Holland defeated Australia in a one-day match at The Hague in 1964. Australia batted poorly, with only Norm O'Neill (87) making more than 20 runs. However, Jack Potter could not complete his innings after having his skull fractured by a ball from Ben Trijzelaar.

Maiden bowled

The British tabloid press had a field day in 1996 when there was a report that a village club was boasting a new trophy - a pair of women's panties. When members of the Guisborough Cricket Club went to investigate movement under a tarpaulin, they came across a couple making love.

Caught in slips, so to speak, the couple grabbed their clothes and took off - the woman leaving her knickers behind. One Fleet Street newspaper headlined the incident: MAIDEN BOWLED - AND CAUGHT!

Retired tired

Former Australian batsman Peter Burge was a prodigy who, as a 13-year-old, hit a double century, six centuries and a 99 in 10 innings. The scorebook for his double century recorded that he had "retired tired".

Graceless

Australian Billy Murdoch had the perfect reply when Dr W.G. Grace started boasting of his batting ability. When Dr Grace asked Murdoch how many great batsmen he had bowled to, Murdoch replied: "One less than you think."

Missing the missus

This tale about West Indies batting legend Viv Richards in a match for Somerset is apocryphal. It is claimed that after smashing a massive six into the crowd, a fan later complained to Richards: "You should be more careful. You only just missed hitting my wife."

Richards is reported to have replied: "I'm awfully sorry."

The ultimate fan

A report from England in 1996 suggested that cricket fan Eddie Baxter, 60, had committed suicide because he could not stand the boredom of winter. He was diagnosed as having an illness described as "seasonal affective disorder".

No-balled!

South African batsman Clive Rice created a storm in 1980 when he appeared nude in the sports pages of a Johannesburg newspaper. The photograph showed Rice reclining, wearing only a St Christopher's medal and a cricket bat placed strategically to stump readers.

Rice, whose pose advertised cricket clothing, defended himself by saying: "I don't care what they say. If the criticism is negative, that is also good, because an advertisement must grab attention."

The Don versus the rest

And, on the question of advertisements, a hoarding promoting a Sheffield Shield match in 1936 had the banner headline: BRADMAN. In small pint underneath, there was reference to the match itself, Queensland versus South Australia.

A battle of tactics

The shrewdness of Don Bradman was illustrated by an incident in a Test against England at the MCG in 1937. The wicket was badly affected by rain and England struggled to 9/76. England captain Gubby Allen had had enough and several Australian fieldsman heard him say "I've had it" before walking off with partner Bill Voce.

Bradman asked umpire if George Borwick if Allen had declared the England innings closed. Borwick had to go to the England dressing room to confirm the declaration and this added four minutes to the authorised 10 minute interval between innings.

Bradman obviously had been buying time to allow the wicket to dry and then, when the Australians batted, the order was reversed so that the wicket would be more playable when the top order faced the England bowling. Australia went on to win by 365 runs.

The English newspaper, *The Daily Telegraph*, carried this report on the great battle of tactics:

"After the dismissal of Hammond in the first innings, the batsmen evidently received instructions to throw away their wickets, but at the same time to disguise their intentions. The order was carried out with some considerable degree of subtlety until Verity, coming in, disclosed the secret by meeting Hardstaff half-way to the wicket.

"Australia then wished to keep England in so that they would not be obliged to bat again on the same wicket. But Allen blocked the plan by declaring when the Australian bowlers were deliberately bowling wides to waste time. More subtle methods must be adopted if Australia expect to outwit players with greater experience of rain-damaged wickets.

"Allen's effort to get an advantage was spoiled by bad light and rain. He would have gained more ground had he applied the closure after the fall of Hammond's wicket, thereby giving Australia an hour to bat and frustrating Bradman's reply of using tail-enders."

Want a bet?

Australian all-rounder Keith Miller, a knockabout sort of character who always has called a spade a bloody shovel, must have been the ultimate cricket realist.

After England spinner Jim Laker had cast a spell over the Australians in the first innings of the Fourth Test at Old Trafford in 1956, Australian skipper Ian Johnson called his team together before its second innings.

The Australians trailed by 375 and, with Laker spinning the ball almost at right angles (he took nine wickets in Australia's first innings), the task looked hopeless. Johnson refused to concede defeat and gave his team a pep talk, telling them it was possible to save the Test with a combination of courage, determination and concentration.

The laconic Miller, sitting in a corner of the Australian dressing room, waited for Johnson to finish his pep talk to say: "I'll give you 6/4 to say we can't save the Test."

Run out - by a snake

A strong, hot northerley wind blew straight down the ground to make conditions for cricket almost unbearable. The temperature hovered around 40 degrees Celsius and batsmen and fielders tried to conserve energy as best they could.

However, batsman Damian Glass, playing for the Victorian town of Yackandandah against Kiewa in the 1996-7 season, found energy he did not know he had when taking off for a quick single.

As he ambled through for his run, he almost stumbled on to a three-metre brown snake. Glass, in panic, tried to accelerate, but slipped and was run out. It is not recorded what happened to the pitch invader.

The good sport

Australian all-rounder Keith Miller proved his sportsmanship in a Test against the West Indies at Bridgetown in 1955 when West Indies skipper Denis Atkinson walked down the wicket to talk to his batting partner.

Atkinson mistakenly believed the ball was "dead" and although Miller knew he could run out the Windies skipper, simply turned to Atkinson and warned him: "You know I could run you out." Atkinson went on to make 219 before being bowled by Richie Benaud, sharing a seventh-wicket partnership of 347 with wick-etkeeper Clairemont dePeiza. The Test was drawn.

The nervous nineties

It is one of the quirks of cricketing statistics that the legendary Don Bradman was never dismissed in the nervous 90s in his long and illustrious Test career. This in itself reflects his enormous ability to withstand pressure. However, many other batsmen have not been so fortunate and the record books are thick with the names of those dismissed in the 90s.

Australia's Dirk Wellham certainly went through agony against England in his Test debut at The Oval before eliminating his name from the list. Wellham, a decade later, recalled the circumstances surrounding his experience of the Test nervous 90s:

Don Bradman - *could take pressure*

"I had raced from the 60s to the 90s as the word came out that we were going to push it along for a declaration on the fourth afternoon of the Sixth Test. The combination of a player in his first Test to score a century and the appearance of a thick, dark cloud over the ground caused our captain Kim Hughes to send a message that I could take my time.

"I was on 99 for 25 minutes, agonising over every missed chance to push the ball through a ringed infield. After I had been on 99 for 15 minutes, the drinks break came and brought some relief from the seemingly endless tension. I drank, chatted about nothing and returned to pick up my bat and began to pull on the gloves.

"As I composed myself to continue, a voice from nearby said: 'You've done all the hard work, don't throw it away now."

It was England bowler Ian Botham, who had been straining to dismiss the Australian batsman to deny him his moment of glory.

Wellham continued: "Ten minutes after resumption, my instincts took over and I punched a shortish delivery through to the cover boundary." Wellham was dismissed soon after for 103.

A runner, and crutches

Spectators at a Castle Cup match in South Africa in 1994 could hardly believe their eyes when Eastern Province number 11 Rowan Lyle made his way to the crease - on crutches with a leg in plaster. Of course, he also had a runner, who carried Lyle's bat to the crease.

Lyle, who had broken a toe earlier in the match against Transvaal, had to discard the crutches to bat. But, in great pain, he shared a last-wicket stand of 23 to help Eastern Province avoid defeat.

And, talking of courage, what about the efforts of Queenslander Pat Reid, who defied doctors orders by continuing to play cricket after he had lost both legs below the knees in a railway accident?

A top junior in Townsville, Reid took a wicket and scored 30 runs in three matches after being invited to play in the 1990 Charters Towers Goldfield Ashes carnival. He was quoted as saying: "I thought I was stuffed for life when the accident occurred but it was great to get a chance to play the game again."

The sabotaged Test

The Third Test of the 1975 Ashes series was abandoned after the pitch was sabotaged overnight before the final day's play. When Headlingley groundsman George Cawthray removed the covers he was aghast. Holes had been dig into the wicket and oil had been poured to make repairs impossible.

The vandalism was part of a publicity campaign for the release of convicted armed robber George Davis, who was serving a 20-year sentence. English cricket fans immediately went into mourning as the odds were in favor of England, with Australia needing 225 runs for victory and only seven wickets in hand.

Radio commentator and former England fast bowler Fred Trueman was angry enough to suggest: "I'd thrown them (the saboteurs) off the top of the pavilion. Mind, I'm a fair man and I'd give them a 50-50 chance. I'd have (England cricketer and a notoriously poor catcher) Keith Fletcher underneath trying to catch them."

Ironically, a man named Peter Chappell was sentenced to nine months' jail for damage to the Headlingley wicket. And Australia's captain for that Test was Ian Chappell!

The Australian Test captain, years later in the book *Ashes Battles and Bellylaughs*, recalled that team manager Fred Bennett rang him early in the morning to tell him the pitch had been sabotaged.

Chappell, who had been dismissed the previous day, wrote: "'Piss off, Fred', I said...'I don't need practical jokes at this hour. What I need is more sleep.'"

"'It's not a joke, Ian. I'll see you downstairs in two minutes.'

".......so I grabbed the clothes that were draped over a chair, slipped my feet into a pair of sandals and headed for the door. When I arrived downstairs it became obvious that Fred was serious, but there was no time to change. To make matters worse, when I arrived at the ground there were a lot of photographers gathered around the damaged pitch.

"And that's how I came to be photographed in a pair of slacks, open-necked shirt, and a sweater and only a pair of Adidas slip-ons on my feet, while (England captain) Tony Greig is immaculate in sportscoat, slacks, tie, shoes and socks."

One ball, one duck

Victorian leg-spinner Jim Higgs had the "distinction" of failing to score a single run on the 1975 Ashes tour of England. In fact, he faced just one delivery - and was bowled for a golden duck by Chris Balderstone in a match against Leicestershire.

We want Bradman!

Victorian pace bowler Harry "Bull" Alexander often was heard to boast that he twice had dismissed the great Don Bradman and then moan that it should have been three dismissals.

Alexander recalled years later of the time he bowled to Bradman in the Victoria-New South Wales Sheffield Shield match at the MCG in 1929, with Bradman 85 not out at lunch: "He hooked me for four straight after lunch and my reaction was to give one ball everything and pitch it up further.

"He tried the shot again and the ball took his leg 'dolly' clean out of the ground. There was an enormous roar at that. It was one of the only two times I ever got Bradman out.

"I was denied another chance to have a go at him, though, later in a testimonial match. I had quickly dismissed openers Bill Ponsford and Archie Jackson. When Bradman came in, Jack Ryder took me off.

"He said he didn't want Bradman dismissed before lunch because it would affect the gate takings. He survived until then and, sure enough, after the interval the crowd had grown by about 20,000."

Cricket all the rage

A cricket captain named Young created headlines of the wrong type in 1961 when he was sentenced to two months' jail after being convicted of striking an umpire in a scratch match between two Melbourne hotels.

Glory, glory, glory

The mood in England following its Ashes triumph in Australia in 1970-1 was, to say the least, jubilant. One Fleet Street newspaper ran the banner headline "GLORY, GLORY, GLORY" and BBC commentator Brian Johnston decided that it was time the cricket world should follow the soccer tradition of national songs to celebrate victory.

Just months earlier, the 1970 England World Cup soccer team hit number one on the charts with *Back Home.* Johnston therefore came up with the following, with music by jazz identity Vic Lewis:

We've brought the Ashes back home
We've got them here in the urn
The Aussies had had them 12 years
So it was about our turn
But oh! What a tough fight
It's been in the dazzling sunlight
In spite of the boos of the mob on the Hill
We've won by two matches to nil.

When we arrived people said
The Aussies would leave us for dead
But we knew we would prove them wrong
And that's why we're singing this song
Oh! The feeling is great
For losing is something we hate
So Sydney we thank you for both of our wins
But not for those bottles and tins.

Our openers gave us a good start
And the others then all played their part
We usually made a good score
Seven times three hundred or more
The Aussies, however, were apt
To collapse at the drop of a hat
If they were bowled any ball that was short
It was 10 to one on they'd be caught.

In the field it was often too hot
So sometimes we felt very low
Whether rain was forecast or not
We always knew we'd have Snow
So now to go home we are free
And we're sure the Aussies agree
Though the series has been a long uphill climb
We've all had a real bumper time."

Caught, at the wicket

A batsman in a match at Eton in 1957 was dismissed in the most bizarre circumstances. He snicked a ball into the wicketkeeper's gloves and, joy of joys, watched as it bobbled out of the gloves.

Then, horror of horrors, he watched as the ball wedged itself between the off and middle stumps. The wicketkeeper, obviously a quick thinker, pulled the ball from between the stumps and appealed for a catch. The batsman was given out. After all, the ball had not hit the ground.

A dull gull

A seagull cost a junior batsman a century in a match in Melbourne during the 1994-5 season. Blair Sellers, batting for South Melbourne, timed a shot superbly, only to see the ball cannon into a seagull.

The ball pulled up short and Sellers took just two runs after being denied an almost certain boundary. He later was dismissed for 98. The bird's fate was not reported.

A handy over

A batsman named Kurt Jansen smashed 41 runs from one over in a match for Northolt against Ealing in England in 1987. The over included two no balls and Jansen hit six sixes, a four and - to keep the strike - a single off the last ball.

Lillee the slowie

Former umpire Robin Bailhache tells a good story about the time the great Dennis Lillee toiled away for little effort on a dry, flat wicket against the West Indies at Brisbane's Gabba in 1979. Lillee, the fast bowling terror of the time, just could not get any life from the docile wicket.

His shirt was soaked with sweat as he kept toiling away until, finally, he pulled up to catch breath at the end of yet another unproductive over. As he took his hat from Bailhache he remarked: "Geez, it's hard being a fast bowler. I ought to know; I used to be one."

Extra, extra, extra long-off

Author Richard Gordon - famous for his *Doctor* series - once remarked that he was the world's greatest cricket fan and the world's worst cricketer. In fact, he often used to tell anyone who would listen that when he played in one match the captain "hid" him on the edge of the field by asking him to stand behind a tree.

An umpire's ton

Joseph Filliston won fame as the oldest man to umpire a match at Lord's. Filliston was 100 years of age when he stood in the Lord's Taverners versus Old England match in 1962. He was killed two years later when hit by a motor scooter.

Damn Yankees!

Incredible as it might seem, a match between Australian and American servicemen was played in Brisbane in 1943, and here is an account of that match, by the Australian captain, John Laffin:

"During the war of 1939-45, we Australian cricketers played the game as best we could, where we could and sometimes against unlikely opponents. For members of the AIF (Australian Imperial Forces), this meant games on desert, rough ground and even on long grass in jungle clearings on the Pacific islands.

"Tens of thousands of American servicemen were in Australia for the Pacific campaign and on one occasion, in Brisbane, the American Army challenged us to a game of cricket. They had been studying it, they said, and it didn't seem very different from baseball; a good eye was apparently the one essential.

"I captained the AIF team and the match took place at the Gabba, the famous Test ground, late in 1943. The Americans batted first and I opened the bowling with leg-spin, with the wicketkeeper standing right up.

"Their opener made fearsome swipes at the first five balls and missed each time. He was obviously tense, his partner at the other end was saying irritably, 'For Chrissake Harvey, why don't you HIT it?' and the 'keeper was expectant.

"I bowled the sixth ball. So much happened within a few seconds that it was difficult even then to be clear about the sequence of events, and looking back, I am still not sure. It was something like this.

"The Yank stepped aside and swiped ferociously. He connected and skied the ball directly over the 'keeper's head. Then he threw down his bat, baseball style, and began to race along the pitch screaming, 'Goddam Marvin, I hit it!' The flying bat knocked a stump and sent it sideways.

"The 'keeper, not normally a phlegmatic man but now excited by the American's tension, caught the ball just above the stumps, though as he said later he was not sure whether it had come off bat, pad or boot. Seeing the batsman out of his crease he wrenched up a stump for good measure.

"The 'keeper and I appealed; the rest of the team were staggering or lying about the field in uncontrollable laughter. Up went the umpire's finger, but nobody was sure for what precise reason.

"Back at the pavilion we looked at 'how out'. The scorer had at first put 'bowled Laffin, caught Cartwright (the 'keeper'); this had been half rubbed out and replaced with 'bowled Laffin and stumped Cartwright'; and this in turn had become 'hit wicket'.

"There was even a school of thought which held the fact that in fact the Yank had been run out since he had long since completed the stroke which could have led to his being stumped.

"I turned to the umpire, 'Well, how WAS he out?'

"'Multiple suicide,' he said.

"The match itself was a bit like a multiple suicide. Those Americans really did have good eyes and when they connected, the ball travelled high and far. Most of them hit at least one six and all of them fell to spin.

"Unable to get the hang of bowling, they consistently threw - they just couldn't help it - so we legalised throwing for the duration of the match, provided the ball hit the ground first.

"On that hard Gabba surface it really climbed sharply. When I shook hands with the Yank skipper after our victory he said, 'Your win, Aussie, fair and square. How would you like to take us on at baseball?'

"We did - but that's another story."

"The big ship" in dock

Australian Test captain Warwick "The Big Ship" Armstrong was his own man and, apart from being a wonderful leader, was always keen to prick pomposity and the inflexibility of officialdom, as illustrated by an incident on the 1921 tour of England.

Armstrong was concerned about the hectic schedule organised for the Australian team and asked team manager Sydney Smith if the program could be re-arranged so that the Australians could have a day's rest before a Test.

The Australians were playing Yorkshire at that particular time and the Yorkshire committee rejected Armstrong's request out of hand, insisting that the tour arrangements had been made even before the Australians had sailed for England.

Armstrong therefore made his own protest in the final Test of the series by using batsmen "Nip" Pellew and Johnny Taylor as bowlers while he read a newspaper in the outfield.

Want a bet, m'lord?

Warwick Armstrong was quite a character and did not brook interference, from anyone. For example, he once suggested that Test umpires in England be paid: "As there is a lot of betting in Tests, it would be wise to remove them from temptation."

Warwick Armstrong - a rest in the outfield

Lord Harris, a great English cricket identity, was shocked and insisted: "People don't bet on cricket."

To which Armstrong retorted: "If you'd like 500 pounds on the next Test, m'Lord, I can get it on for you."

Down and out

This tale might not be true, but it was recorded in Lillywhite's *Scores and Biographies* that when nineteenth century NSW and Australian fast bowler Charlie Turner hit a ball into the air in a

Sheffield Shield match last century, a fieldsman accidentally dropped his trousers in reaching to take a catch.

The fieldsman desperately clutched at the trouser's waist-band, only to juggle the ball. Then, in re-claiming the ball his trousers fell around his ankles.

Hail this storm!

Australian batsman Sid Barnes had a wonderful sense of humor, as the England tourists discovered during a match at the Gabba, Brisbane, in 1946. Play was stopped when a storm dumped massive hailstones onto the ground. The Englishmen could not believe their eyes, as the hailstones were as big as golf balls.

Barnes told the tourists that this was nothing as he had seen much bigger hailstones and even suggested that some he had seen later had been used in ice-chests. The Englishmen, naturally, did not believe him, so Barnes set out to show them just how big hailstones could be in Australia.

Barnes, at the height of the storm, raided the bar and produced a massive block of ice and then chucked it over the pavilion roof. "There," he said. "That's how big they are in Australia."

Barnes might have been able to get away with this stunt, except that one of the tourists was suspicious of the square edges on the "hailstone".

Gee, that was close!

Believe it or not, the tied Australia-West Indies Test at the Gabba in 1960 was so tense that Australian Ken "Slasher" Mackay asked teammate Norman O'Neill in the dressing room: "Who won?"

Bowled over

Cambridge University wicketkeeper Nathaniel Hone "drew stumps" in the most unfortunate circumstances last century. He went to a chemist's shop to complain about being ill and was given a medicine to drink.

Unfortunately, however, the chemist mistakenly gave him a dose of carbolic acid and Hone died a few hours later.

A lesson from the master

During a South Australia-New South Wales Sheffield Shield match in Adelaide in the '50s, dashing SA batsman Les Favell played such a magnificent shot on his way to a century that teammate Barry Jarman exclaimed: "I wish I could play a cover-drive like that."

Immediately, from behind an open door, he heard Sir Donald Bradman say: "If you got your feet closer to the ball, you would."

The prophet

Billy Murdoch, a great Australian batsman, literally lived and died for cricket. A Test star from 1877, he scored the first Test double century in making 211 at The Oval in 1884. After captaining Australia in 1890, he moved to England then represented England against South Africa in one Test in 1891-2.

Dedicated to the great game, he watched cricket as often as possible following his retirement and was at the MCG when Australia played South Africa in 1911. After Australia made 328 in its first innings very early on the second day, Murdoch told friends that he believed five South African wickets would fall before lunch.

Billy Murdoch - a prophet

Murdoch must have been a brilliant judge of cricket because Australia did crash through the early South African wickets to take five wickets before lunch and this prompted Murdoch to say: "I'll never make a prophecy again. I've brought bad luck on those boys."

Murdoch indeed was a prophet as he almost immediately had a stroke and died later in hospital, at just 56 years of age. Australia went on to win the Test by 530 runs, with flags at the MCG lowered to half-mast.

A break in play

The late Lindsay Hassett, a great Australian batsman and Test captain, liked to tell the tale of how experience can save the day and it is must be the ultimate tale of how to delay play to avoid defeat.

As Hassett used to tell the tale, his District club of South Melbourne was playing a match against University at the Lakeside Oval in the '30s and dismissed the Students cheaply in their first innings.

Then, when South Melbourne was due to bat, rain intervened. This was a blessing as the wicket was wicked. Unfortunately for South Melbourne, however, the sky cleared and the umpires declared that play could resume.

With just an hour to stumps and play set to resume the following weekend, the South players knew it would be almost impossible to preserve wickets and therefore resorted to delaying tactics.

Batsmen would wander down the wicket to pat down a piece of turf or hold mid-wicket conferences. A couple of wickets fell and it was the wily old captain's turn to take the crease. And, as he took block, he had one eye on the pavilion clock.

He bent to tie a bootlace, went down to talk to his batting partner and, after wasting at least four minutes, faced the first ball. The infuriated University bowler worked up a good head of steam and the ball flew off the pitch and thumped into the skipper's gloves.

The skipper howled in pain and rage, threw his glove to the ground and examined his hand. Surely it was broken, or at least badly bruised? He called for the team trainer, who took the field to examine his captain's injury. Minutes ticked by while the wounded hand was taped. But it was not enough. There were still five minutes to play.

Umpires ordered the resumption of play and, as the skipper bent over his bat, a band playing at a motor racing carnival around the Lakeside Oval struck up *God Save The King to* mark the end of the day's racing.

The battle-smart skipper dropped his bat, stood to attention and started singing the then national anthem. By the time the band had stopped playing the clock had ticked past six o'clock - and stumps. Experience and rat-like cunning had allowed the South Melbourne skipper to face just one ball in half an hour.

Unfortunately, however, Hassett could never remember the final result. Still, it's a good yarn!

Death of a legend

Followers of the Australian Football League competition would be aware that the founders of the Australian code were Henry Harrison and Thomas Wills. However, few football fans know that Wills also was a great cricket identity and, indeed, one of the best cricketers of his era and, at one stage, was Melbourne Cricket Club secretary.

Sadly, Wills drifted into alcoholism and stabbed himself to death with a pair of scissors on May 2, 1880. Although many other cricket identities have suicided over the years, Wills' death surely ranks as particularly tragic.

Noted Australian historian Geoffrey Blainey, in his *A Game Of Our Own*, a history of Australian football's earliest years, wrote of Wills:

"Every Victorian reader interested in cricket knew that a fast, low ball from Tommy Wills would rattle their ankles. In all the land perhaps no cricketer was held in more affection by the crowd, and he was almost 38 when his name was widely discussed as a possible player against W.G. Grace's visiting English team.

"By then, alas, a certain unreliability on and off the field virtually debarred him. Hundreds of cricket followers in Melbourne had hoped that he would be selected and *The Australian Sketcher* movingly wrote in November 1873 of the loyalty he still commanded.

"The public view of him was almost adoring: 'With all thy faults I love thee still, Tommy Wills'. In that era when the title of Mister was courteously extended to most men who batted or marked or rowed, he was one of the few Victorian sportsmen to be known widely not by his surname, but his Christian name. He was 'Tommy'. Everyone knew who Tommy was.

"Tommy's last years were a long mishap. In later photographs of him standing with fellow cricketers, he conveys a touch of the hippy. The bottle was not far away whenever he returned to the cricket pavilion. Becoming an alcoholic, he was placed in the care of a strong male attendant at his Heidelberg home. At lunchtime on May 2, 1880, for the moment unattended, he seized a pair of scissors.

"His wife saw his intention but did not have the strength to prevent him from stabbing himself three times in the breast. He died that afternoon, aged 44.

"He was buried on the hilltop at Heidelberg, overlooking that green valley which Streeton and Roberts and the painters of the Heidelberg School eight years later would depict in summer colours.

"A third generation Australian - then a rarity - he had often expressed in football and cricket a version of the national feeling which these artists were to express with paint, and he had been quietly proud that the football game he did so much to shape was called 'the national game'."

One-wicket wonder

New Zealand bowler Horace Smith holds the bizarre record of taking a wicket with his first ball in Test cricket, yet never taking another wicket. Smith took his wicket against England at Christchurch in 1932-3 when he bowled Eddie Paynter. However, he sent down another 119 balls without success in that match and never played Test cricket again.

No need to bat

A team playing in the York Senior League in 1979 won a match without one of its batsmen scoring a single run. This unique feat was achieved by the Cawood team dismissing Dringhouses for just two runs. Then, when Dringhouses bowled, the first ball went for four byes.

Getting his goat

When the colorful Nawab of Pataudi toured Australia with the England team in 1932-3, he won fans with his wit in an exchange with a notorious barracker at the SCG. The barracker called out to Pataudi: "Hello, Mr Ghandi, where's your goat?"

As quick as a flash, Pataudi replied: "He has broken his rope and got into the crowd."

ould kill

...ralian captain and MCC secretary Ian Johnson had ...te yarn from the 1955 tour of West Indies about a match played near a local prison in Antigua. Johnson often has told how the prisoners not only prepared the wicket, but were allowed to watch the match.

Every time Australian pace bowler Keith Miller charged in, they would chant: "Bowl him a bumper, bowl him a bumper." The cricket-loving prisoners apparently wanted to see blood on the wicket.

Miller, between overs, decided to have a chat with one of the prisoners and asked: "What did you do to be in prison?"

The prisoner replied: "I got 20 years for murdering my wife and I want you to bowl another bumper."

Miller could not wait to start his next over.

Horse of a different kind

Although this tale is apocryphal, it is worth telling as it covers both cricket and horse-racing. It concerns Australian batsman Edgar Mayne during the 1912 tour of England when the Australian team was entertained "at home" by the Duke of Portland.

Mayne spotted a set of mounted horses' hooves and admired them so much he asked the Duke of Portland if he could have one as a souvenir. The duke replied: "The hooves are from a horse, not a bloody centipede."

The famous "Yabba"

Only elderly Australian cricket fans can recall the remarkable barracking of Stephen Gascoigne, better known as Yabba. Possibly the most famous cricket barracker of them all, Yabba plied his trade as amateur commentator from a position in the Hill at the SCG and amused all within earshot.

A huge man with an even bigger voice, Yabba had rare timing as he always managed to come up with a lively comment at the perfect time. One of his regular deliveries was reserved for slow-scoring batsman. When the batsman broke the shackles for a scoring shot Yabba would yell: "Whoa there; he's bolted."

Yabba, despite a rough and ready appearance, was a cricket expert and it was obvious to anyone who ever heard him on his throne at the SCG that he had grown up with and loved the greatest of games. There were suggestions he had followed the game from a very early age.

One of Yabba's most famous comments centred around the Nawab of Pataudi, who took more than half an hour to make a run. Yabba's patience finally expired and he yelled to the umpire, a gas inspector: "Put a penny in him. He's stopped registering."

When Yabba died in 1942, Sydney's Daily Mirror ran the headline: "YABBA, FAMOUS BARRACKER, DIES." The report read:

"Australia's most famous cricket barracker, Yabba, died today in the Lidcombe State Hospital, aged 64.

"Yabba's real name was Stephen Harold Gascoigne. His fame as a barracker spread throughout the world. He had a stentorian voice and a sound and deep knowledge of cricket, although he himself was not a player.

"His favorite rendezvous was 'The Hill' at the Sydney Cricket Ground during big games, which he would enliven with his witty and spontaneous remarks. There was no tedious repetition about Yabba's barracking - a trait unfortunately not possessed by his imitators."

The longest innings

Although this tale also is apocryphal, it is worth telling and concerns former Australian Prime Minister Sir Robert Menzies and his wife Dame Pattie. Of course, Sir Robert was a passionate cricket fan, and Dame Pattie most certainly was not.

Sir Robert and Dame Pattie attended a match at the MCG and watched England's Jack Hobbs and Herbert Sutcliffe bat. Almost two years later, the Menzies attended a match at Lord's, with Hobbs and Sutcliffe again batting. Legend has it that Dame Pattie turned to her husband and remarked: "Haven't we got those two out yet?"

Keeper of the ashes

Australian Test wicketkeeper Hanson Carter surely had one of the most unusual occupations among his peers. Carter, who played 28 Tests before and after World War I, was an undertaker and often attended funerals before standing behind the stumps. Carter, who was born in Yorkshire, was one of the pall-bearers at the funeral of the legendary Victor Trumper in 1915.

Politics and cricket

Victorian all-rounder Sam Loxton ran into political problems during a match for Victoria against New South Wales at the SCG.

Loxton, a Victorian member of parliament, was bowling during a match attended by striking waterside workers.

Every time Loxton ran into bowl, the wharfies would shout abuse and, in return, Loxton would wave encouragement at the end of each delivery.

When Loxton finally took a spell, he went to field at fine leg, where one barracker yelled: "If you're 35 (years of age), Loxton, I'm 25."

Loxton immediately turned to the wharfie and countered: "At least I have a birth certificate to prove it."

Less than average

Although this yarn is apocryphal, it is believed there is some element of truth in it. It concerns the England tour of Australia in 1994-5 when a visiting English journalist asked the great Sir Donald Bradman what he thought he would average against the England attack.

Sir Donald carefully digested the question before answering: "Oh, around 50 or so."

The Englishman replied: "But you averaged almost 100 in your Test career."

"Yes, but I'm now 86 years of age."

Drunk, old bean?

Australian captain Warwick "The Big Ship" Armstrong was a man who plotted his own course, as evidenced by his attitude in 1921 when Victorian officials tried to convince the rest of the cricket world that, at 41 years of age, he was too old to remain in first-class cricket.

The group sought, and won, the Victorian media's support in pushing the view that Armstrong was past his prime, only for The Big Ship to answer them in the best possible way - by scoring 157 not out against the touring England side.

The Victorian bid to "retire" Armstrong not only had failed, but Armstrong led Australia to victory in the first three Tests against England that summer. However, Armstrong injured a leg batting for Australia and he ruled himself unfit for a NSW-Victoria Sheffield Shield clash in Sydney.

Victorian secretary Ernest Bean and one or two other officials did not believe Armstrong was injured, so removed him as Victorian captain, sparking such public outrage in Melbourne that he not only was reinstated but continued in his role as Australian Test captain.

Then, in the Fourth Test of the series, Armstrong had a bout of malaria and dropped himself down the batting order in an effort to recover. A whiskey merchant, Armstrong had a few nips of his best products to steady himself when he went out to bat and saw Bean smirking to himself. It was obvious the Victorian secretary would use Armstrong's drinking as a means of revenge.

Armstrong, one of the most determined batsmen to pull on a baggy green cap, thwarted Bean's plans by thumping 123 and, when he finally marched back to the pavilion, he passed a drunken Bean - a teetotaller.

A man of many talents

Australian Monty Noble, a star Test batsman of the turn of the century, not only was a brilliant cricketer, but also was a dentist and an excellent writer. His book *The Game's The Thing* is still regarded as a classic. But there's more...Noble also was a fine singer and often sang solo (as a baritone) for the Sydney Choral Society.

A job well done

Former Australian pace bowler Ernie McCormack used to like telling how he thought he had landed himself in trouble after bowling one too many bouncers to a bunny batsman in a tour match against Worcestershire in 1938.

McCormack, who died in 1991, loved telling how, after his "victim" had to be carted off to hospital after having a ball thunder into his skull, the Australian pace man next day had to face the batsman's wife.

"I'm terribly sorry," McCormack apologised. "It was just one of those things. Please forgive me."

"Oh, don't worry about it," the wife replied. "I've been wanting to scone him for years."

First and last?

Ian Craig caused a sensation when he was named in the Australian team for a Test against South Africa in 1952-3. At 17 years of age, he became Australia's youngest ever Test representative.

On the 1953 tour of England, the youngster was introduced to the Queen, who asked him if it was his first tour of England, to which Craig replied:

"Yes, Your Majesty, but unless my batting improves it also will be my last."

A gift for Jardine

Douglas Jardine undoubtedly was the most unpopular England captain to tour Australia. Not only was he seen as the master-mind of the English Bodyline tactics against Australia in 1932-3, but he was regarded by many Australian fans as an upper-class English snob.

Jardine was the subject of abuse almost from the first tour game, against Western Australia in Perth. His cut-glass accent and his insistence on wearing his Harlequin caps were symbols of his alleged sense of superiority.

Australian fans therefore took great delight in trying to bring Jardine back to earth, as evidenced by one incident in Adelaide when a horse relieved itself after having drawn a roller for the pitch.

As a workman shovelled the horse manure from the wicket area, a wag in the crowd yelled out: "Give it to Jardine." Earlier, Jardine had insisted that the gates to the Adelaide Oval be shut to prevent fans from watching the English team practice at the nets. The move infuriated the South Australian public almost as much as the Bodyline tactics designed to restrict the great Don Bradman.

Your drinks, sirs

Australian Test batsman Sid Barnes created headlines during the summer of 1952-3 when he played the butler for the New South Wales team during a Sheffield Shield match against South

Australia in Adelaide. But Barnes' bizarre appearance was just the end-piece of one of the most dramatic chapters in Australian cricket history.

Barnes, usually described as a "rough diamond" or "a boy from the wrong side of the tracks", often was in trouble with cricket authorities for one petty misdemeanor or another, from jumping the turnstiles when refused admittance - despite being one of Australia's most famous sports identities - to bowing to heckling crowds in England.

Matters came to a head in December 1951, when the Australian Board of Control refused to ratify the Australian selectors' team for a Test against the West Indies. The team was referred back to the selectors because of an objection to one player's inclusion. And everyone knew the player concerned was Barnes.

Rumors flew thick and fast over Barnes' exclusion and the matter became the subject of a national debate. What was the offence and should Barnes have been dumped from the side? Barnes sat back helplessly until a letter to a Sydney newspaper suggested that "the board would not have excluded Mr Barnes from an Australian Eleven capriciously, but only for a matter of a sufficiently serious matter."

Barnes sued the letter writer for libel and, at a

subseqent court hearing, it was disclosed that Barnes had been excluded because he had taken (movie) films during the 1948 Australian tour of England. These movies included shots of the Royal Family, without permission.

Barnes won his case but, after failing to win a place in the Australian team for a Test against South Africa in 1952, realised he would never win back his place. He was 36 years of age and decided on a dramatic step. Barnes suggested he be dropped from the NSW team for the match against South Australia and that he act as twelfth man.

The NSW selectors agreed with this request/suggestion and Barnes took the field during a drinks break wearing a double-breasted lounge suit, a snappy tie, a red carnation in the suit buttonhole and, of all things, carrying a portable radio.

Barnes had made his point and, to a certain extent, had the last laugh. Tragically, he died of a sleeping pill overdose in 1973.

Dog of a night

The late Bill O'Reilly, one of the greatest bowlers the game has seen, used to like telling the story of how he and fellow Australians Bill Fingleton and Arthur Morris once were invited to the London home of England batsman Denis Compton.

Compton's wife Valerie made a great fuss of their two dogs, yappy little Maltese terriers. These dogs obviously were the Compton's pride and joy as both were immaculately groomed, sported bright ribbons and had the run of the home.

When O'Reilly was invited to pat the dogs, he reached out and had his hand bitten. The Comptons were horrified but, while they left the room in search of a bandage, O'Reilley lashed out and kicked the dog across the room.

Years later, Morris told his host what had happened and Compton replied: "I wish I'd known. I hated those bloody dogs."

A wily old skipper

Herbert Collins was one of the shrewdest men ever to captain Australia and was renowned for his luck in winning the toss. He went by the nickname "Horseshoe", but it is not known whether this had anything to do with horse-racing and his love of a punt or for some other obscure reason. Besides, he also was known as "Nutty", probably because he was a tough nut to crack.

Regardless, Collins played it hard and tough as the Australian skipper. His flinty-eyed stare intimidated many an opposition batsman and he knew precisely how to handle the various characters in his own team, as evidenced by an incident when he captained an Australian Infantry Forces Eleven in England in 1919.

During a match against the South of England at Portsmouth, Collins asked wicketkeeper Bert Oldfield to stand at the stumps to an over from fast bowler Jack Gregory. Oldfield could not understand why Collins would make this request, so protested.

Collins insisted on the move, even though Oldfield complained that he would be taking his life into his own hands standing up to such a fast bowler. Collins refused to listen to this line of argument and walked away.

Gregory was infuriated when he saw Oldfield standing up to the stumps and tore in like a maniac. He took a wicket almost immediately and then routed the local team. Collins' tactic of embarrassing Gregory into bowling faster worked a treat.

And there was method in his madness, as he was desperate to catch an early train to England, possibly for a stint at a baccarat table.

Text-book cricket

Although this is one of the best-known yarns in cricket, it is worth repeating here as it illustrates the strong bond between Australian and English cricketers, despite what might happen on the field of combat.

England pace bowler Alec Bedser always seemed to have the better of Australian batsman Arthur Morris and, after dismissing him on his 29th birthday (January 19) in 1951, Bedser sent him a present - a cricket textbook titled *Better Cricket*. With it was a note saying: "I hope you'll like this birthday present, Arthur. It may help you."

But, in the next Test, Morris hit a double century and then returned the book - with the chapter on bowling marked for Bedser's benefit.

On fire in the outfield

Believe it or not, Australia's Arthur Coningham was so cold during a tour match at Blackpool in 1897 that he collected straw and twigs and lit a fire in the outfield to keep warm. Coningham, it would seem, was quite a character but, tragically, spent time in jail for fraud and died in an asylum in 1939.

Coningham played just one Test for Australia - against England at the MCG in 1894-5 - and took a wicket with his first ball. He finished the England first innings with 2/17, but did not take a wicket in conceding 59 runs in the second innings.

Coningham was the centre of enormous controversy in 1899 when he sued his wife on the grounds of adultery with a Roman Catholic priest.

Plain language

Australian cricket writer Claude Corbett was a man who could not be intimidated and, least of all, by any English cricketer. After Corbett complained about England captain Douglas Jardine taking his team onto the ground late for a match against South Australia at the Adelaide Oval in 1932-3, he was summoned before England manager Pelham "Plum" Warner.

Corbett was asked to discuss his complaint and there even was a suggestion that he should apologise, to which he replied: "Go and get #%@ ^ !**"

A right royal greeting

Australian fast bowler Ern Jones was quite a character. A garbage collector, he was a bit of a rough diamond who spoke his mind and did not mind cracking a joke at the expense of authority.

The heavily-moustachoed Jones - or "Jonah" to teammates and cricket fans - once was introduced to a very young Prince of Wales during a tour of England and officials were horrified when the future king of England walked away with what appeared to be tears in his eyes.

Puzzled, the officials raced over to Jones to ask him if there was any explanation for the prince's obvious anguish, to which Jones replied:

"I made up my mind that if I ever got the opportunity to shake hands with the prince, each of us would have good cause to remember it."

The cool of the shade

This tale almost certainly is apocryphal, but is worth a place here because it has gone down in cricket folklore. It concerns Warwick "The Big Ship" Armstrong, the Australian captain who weighed in at more than 20 stone (127kg in modern terminology).

The story is that when Australia was playing against a County side in 1921, a boy kept following Armstrong around the ground. The exasperated Australian captain finally turned to the boy and asked: "Do you want my autograph?"

"No," the boy replied. "I haven't got an autograph book."

"Tibby" Cotter - killed in action

"Well, what do you want?" Armstrong asked.

"Please sir, it's hot and you're the only decent bit of shade in the place."

Death of a hero

Albert "Tibby" Cotter, who played 21 Tests for Australia before World War I, was one of the most feared fast bowlers of his time and, although wayward, was capable of ripping through the best of line-ups when on target.

Cotter played the first of his Tests in the 1903-4 series against England but, by the time he had enlisted in the Australian Infantry Forces, had not played Test cricket for at least five years.

It is possible to imagine the surprise - and shock - when an Australian army side played a cricket match against a team of officers in Palestine. Cotter was far too fast for the Englishmen, who claimed they had never faced anything like his fast bowling. If only they had known their adversary was a man who had taken seven wickets in a Test innings at The Oval in 1907.

Tragically, Cotter was killed by a sniper's bullet at Beersheba, Palestine, on October 31, 1917. He was just 32 years of age. It has been suggested that Cotter's last words, to a mate after being mortally wounded, were: "Blue, you can have the fish supper on your own."

Taken to the cleaners

Australian opening batsman Lindsay Hassett did not bat an eyelid when a waiter at a posh London hotel dropped a plate of ice-cream onto the dapper little man's jacket. Unruffled, Hassett merely removed his jacket and handed it to the waiter for cleaning.

Then, after noticing that the ice-cream had also been spilt into his lap, Hassett pushed himself further into the table and unobtrusively removed his trousers. "Here, you take these to the cleaners, too," Hassett told the startled waiter, and continued with his meal.

The PM's dinners

Former Australian Prime Minister Sir Robert Menzies, a lover of cricket, established a great tradition with his selection of Australian Elevens to play touring sides in Canberra, and always made a point of entertaining his guests.

During a speech at a dinner, Sir Robert told guests: "When I was Prime Minister I used to invite both teams to a dinner at the Hotel Canberra."

To which Lindsay Hassett interjected: "And mighty frugal do's they were, too."

The news of the day

When the great Don Bradman was dismissed for 232 in the Fifth Test at The Oval in 1930, English newspaper *The Star* ran a special news poster telling readers in the simplest possible terms: "He's Out."

The wrong score

The old Melbourne Cricket ground scoreboard, replaced in the early '80s by one showing instant electronic replays, was world famous for its ability to allow fans a comprehensive guide to whatever match was being played.

Dean Jones -
beyond the call of duty

However, the scoreboard once was criticised by an American newspaper in the mistaken belief that the facts and figures on hand represented a "totaliser gambling machine".

Correct weight

Australian batsman Dean Jones lost more than seven kilograms in scoring 210 in ferocious, furnace-like heat in the First Test against India at Madras in 1986. He vomited no less than 15 times and hallucinated.

When Jones complained that he could not continue, Australian captain Allan Border threatened he would replace him with a "real Australian". Jones batted beyond the call of duty to play an important role in the tied Test, only the second in cricket history - after the 1960-1 tie between Australia and the West Indies in Brisbane.

The Madras tie was clinched when a delivery from Australia's Greg Matthews struck India's Maninder Singh on the pads and he was given out lbw without scoring. The last four Indian wickets fell for just 16 runs.

A death in the game

Australian pace bowler Ernie McCormick had a reputation for being one of the funniest men to grace the game. There was, for example, the time he was playing at Cape Town in 1935 and asked where he could buy a wreath.

A horrified South African official asked: "Good lord, who's died?"

"No-one," McCormick replied. "I just want to lay it on this pitch (Newlands). It's the deadest thing I've struck."

It was on this tour that McCormick made a famous quip during a tour of the Kimberley diamond mines. When told of the tight security at the mine, which included the examination of workers' stools, McCormick remarked: "I suppose that's where it comes from - the old saying, a flash in the pan."

A fine pair

Australian pace bowler Charles "The Terror" Turner did not earn his nickname for nothing. Successor to Fred "The De-

Charles Turner -
quite a spectacle

George Giffen - home-town hero

mon" Spofforth as Australia's fastest bowler, he made his Test debut in the summer of 1886-7.

It was during that summer that Turner, playing for NSW, bowled England captain Arthur Shrewsbury with a duck in both innings. Turner then presented him with a miniature pair of spectacles.

The one-man team

South Australian George Giffen probably was the most talented Australian cricketer of his era. A splendid batsman, he also was a dangerous medium-pace or off-spin bowler. The idol of Adelaide sports fans, he had a grandstand at the Adelaide Oval named in his honor and was presented with a watch valued at 100 guineas - a huge sum of money at the end of the 19th century.

However, Giffen often was accused of hogging the bowling, even in captaining Australia. In one Test against England, in 1894, teammate Hugh Trumble suggested he remove himself from the attack. Giffen replied: "I think I'll go to the other end."

Giffen bowled 78.2 overs in that innings - far more than any other Australian bowler - but took 6/155 in England's total of 475. England won by 94 runs.

The big upset

Minnow cricket nation Kenya defeated the mighty West Indies during the 1996 World Cup, sparking wild celebrations in the Kenyan city of Nairobi, even though cricket is regarded as a minor sport in the African nation.

Two of the Kenyan heroes, Maurice Odumbe and Steve Tikolo travelled to the United Kingdom to play league cricket in 1991, but were stopped by British immigration officials at Heathrow airport and asked the reason for their visit to the UK.

The officials could hardly believe their ears when Odumbe and Tikolo told them they were on their way to play cricket in, of all places, Wales.

Mean beans

Australian leg-spin star Shane Warne created headlines early in 1998 when he said during a tour of India that he missed eating baked beans. He then was inundated with cans of one of his favorite meals, much to the amusement of the cricket public.

However, Australian physiotherapist Errol Alcott saw a different side to the story when he was contacted by a BBC journalist wanting to get in touch with Warne's tour room-mate.

When the puzzled Alcott asked for an explanation, the journalist replied along the lines: "We want to know what he thinks of Shane eating so many baked beans." We leave this to your imagination...

Lost and found

The entire Queensland population went into raptures when Carl Rackemann took a catch and then threw the ball into the air to give the State its first Sheffield Shield win, in 1994-5. But what happened to the ball?

This was a mystery for three years until Brisbane teenager Sam Handy responded to a newspaper advertisement. It seems he found the ball at his feet when he - along with hundreds of other jubilant fans - invaded the Gabba ground.

Handy presented the ball to Queensland cricket officials and Rackemann was quoted as saying: "Throwing that ball away was one of the dumbest things I have ever done."

A fishy tale

The cricket public has a perception of South African Test captain Hansie Cronje as a dour, humorless character who grinds out the runs and the opposition and, even in victory, finds it difficult to smile.

In reality, the opposite is true. Cronje enjoys a joke more than most cricketers and is regarded by teammates as one of the best practical jokers in world cricket.

For example, there was the time he put a herring in the air-conditioning vent in fast bowler Fanie de Villers' room during a tour of Sri Lanka. It took de Villiers an eternity to discover the cause of the "pong" in his room.

Heads I win, heads you lose

Allan Border, captaining the Prime Minister's Eleven, and West Indies skipper Courtney Walsh found themselves in a dilemma when they went to toss the coin before the start of the traditional match in Canberra in December, 1996.

The Prime Minister, Mr John Howard, gave them a special Sir Donald Bradman $5 coin for the toss. But, when the two captains looked at it, they realised it had a portrait of Sir Donald's head on one side and a portrait of the Queen on the other side. Which side was tails?

As Border said: "Courtney and I worked out which head we'd designate as tails but, by the time the coin landed, I'd forgotten which was which. I'm glad Courtney said 'You've won the toss' because I wasn't sure."

Billy big-ears

During the 1993 Australian tour of England, Steve Waugh and Tim May decided to pull a practical joke at pace bowler Craig "Billy" McDermott's expense.

As McDermott walked back to his bowling mark in a match at Bristol, his Australian teamates all pulled on plastic ears - allegedly similar in size to McDermott's "real" ears - Waugh and May had bought at a joke shop.

Savile row Aussies

During the 1997 tour of South Africa, the Australians decided on a stunt to give themselves a laugh by insisting that they each buy a teammate a ghastly outfit. Names were drawn out of a hat and the lads went to every "oppo" shop they could find.

Then, at a function in East London, they walked through the hotel lobby in the very antithesis of a fashion parade. Jason Gillespie wore a tight brown and orange shirt with a huge collar, Mark Taylor wore a crocheted shirt and Andy Bichel was squeezed into a safari suit at least two sizes too small for him.

Mistaken identity

When pace man Paul Wilson (later to represent Australia) was playing for the Australian Cricket Academy in a match against a Queensland Second Eleven, he decided to sledge an opposition batsman who had snicked several of his deliveries.

"Is this the best Queensland can offer?" he asked.

The batsman was prolific scorer Matthew Hayden, who finished that particular innings with 151 and, a week later, cracked 140 on his Sheffield Shield debut for Queensland and went on to win Australian representative honors.

G'day love!

Australian fast bowler Dennis Lillee made a huge social faux pas during the 1972 Ashes tour when introduced to the Queen. Although he had practised for days on what he would say to the Queen, nerves got the better of him when the Queen offered her hand.

Lillee, who had the very best of intentions, merely said: "G'day".

Cricket corn

The following is a small collection of cricket jokes from around the world. Many, believe it or not, contain more than a kernel of truth.

Not out

A spin bowler sent down one of his most innocuous deliveries and, when the ball plopped into the batsman's pads, he spun around to the umpire and begged the age old cricket question:

"Howzat!"

"Not out," the umpire replied.

"But it didn't deviate and went straight into his pads."

"True."

"He didn't hit the ball before it hit his pads?"

"No."

"Well, why didn't you give him out?"

"Because the ball was not going fast enough to disturb the bails."

ZZZZ!

A cricket fan went to the doctor to complain about insomnia and confessed that he hadn't had a decent night's sleep all summer.

"So how long has it been since you slept right through the night?"

"Oh, about six weeks."

"You mean you haven't had any sleep for six weeks?"

"No, I can sleep through the cricket, but can't get to sleep at night."

Pure hell

A cricket fan died during his sleep and was horrified when St Peter told him he did not qualify for entry and had to go to hell. The cricketer therefore caught the "down" escalator and caught up with Old Nick, who immediately took him to a cricket ground.

The batsmen were in the middle, the fielders were set and the newcomer to hell had to rub his eyes to make sure he was not dreaming. "This isn't hell," he exclaimed. "This is heaven."

"Oh, it's hell all right," Old Nick replied. "There's no ball to play with."

A different point of view

Fans gave umpires hell during most of the day's play, querying almost every decision and criticising them mercilessly. But, just before stumps, the square leg umpire walked from the ground and sat himself among the spectators.

"What do you think you're doing?" one of the fans asked.

"Oh, it's obvious you get a better view from here," the umpire replied.

The young Don

The great Don Bradman was a schoolboy cricket prodigy and, after an under-age match at primary school, his father asked him how he had performed with the bat.

"Oh, all right," the young Don replied. "You have to retire at 50, but I fooled them."

"How's that, son?"

"I got to 49 and then hit a six."

De-railed

A cricketer had a terrible day in the field, dropping no less than four chances. After showering at the end of the day's play, he told his friends that he had better rush to catch his train.

One of his mates drawled: "I hope you have better luck than you did with the ball."

Horses for courses

Play was just about to start in a country match when a horse wandered onto the field and asked the home-team captain if he could have a game.

"Do you bat or bowl?" the captain asked.

"I bat," the horse replied. "And I'm pretty good."

The captain took the horse at his word and opened the batting with the equine cricket wonder. Everyone was amazed as the horse smashed six off every ball in the first over. No-one had seen anything like it.

Then, in the second over, the other opening batsman pushed the ball to cover and called for an easy quick single. He took off, only to see the horse resting on his bat at the other end. The batsman was run out by metres and, as he passed the horse on his way back to the dressing room, he asked testily: "Why didn't you run?"

The horse replied: "If I could run, you nong, I'd be running at Flemington."

A variety of problems

A cricketer went to a doctor to complain about depression and, when asked if he had any idea of the cause of his anxiety, the cricketer replied: "Everything has gone wrong. I can't bat and I can't take a catch."

The doctor then asked if he had thought of giving up cricket and taking up golf.

"I can't," the cricketer replied. "My name's Alec Stewart and I'm the England captain."

Getting settled

The new batsman strode confidently to the wicket, his whites immaculate and his pads in pristine condition. He took block with extreme caution, adjusted the strap on his helmet and, just as he was about to face his first ball, he pulled away to take block again.

He finally settled over his bat, only to have his leg-stump knocked right out of the ground. Bowled for a golden duck! As he made his way back to the pavilion, one of the fieldsmen snapped: "Bad luck, just as you were settling in."

It's his funeral

The office junior asked his boss if he could have the afternoon off to attend his uncle's funeral but, once permission was granted, he marched straight off to the MCG.

He was sitting in the outer, with the score at 0/180, when a finger tapped him on the shoulder and a deep voice asked: "I thought you were going to your uncle's funeral?"

The junior spun around, saw his boss and replied: "It WILL be his funeral. My uncle's bowling."

Different tactics

It was a stinking hot day and the opening bowler's temper didn't improve when he got carted around the ground. The score was 0/84 after just an hour, and time for the captain to make a bowling change.

"Oh, please keep me going," the bowler pleaded. "It's just that the fielders have let me down."

"What do you mean?" the captain asked. "They haven't dropped a single chance."

"Yeah, but I'm not bowling for catches; I'm bowling for run outs."

Boring cricket

The wife of England Test star Trevor "Barnacle" Bailey, noted for his painfully slow batting, went to the doctor to see if there was anything to help her husband relax.

"Here are some sleeping tablets," he told her.

"Do I give these to him the night before the first day's play?" she asked.

"No," the doctor replied. "They're for you while he is batting."

Worth the money

A Lancashire League club employed a West Indies fast bowler as the team professional and, in his first match, he took five wickets in his very first over - without conceding a run. In the second over of the match, the batsmen survived and made just one run.

Then, in the Caribbean star's second over, he again whipped through the line-up to take another five wickets. And, as the players left the field, a fan turned to his mate and suggested: "Gee, that was disappointing for the fans."

To which his mate replied: "Oh, I don't know about that. They got a run for their money."

A change of style

Australia's Merv Hughes had a dreadful match with the ball. He either sprayed deliveries wide or well short of a length and finished the day with 0/100. However, he was determined to find some form and therefore went straight to the nets for practice the next day.

He sent down delivery after delivery and, finally, was convinced he had found his line, length and rhythm. In fact, his nets form was so good he called over Aussie captain Allan Border and asked: "Can you notice any difference?"

To which AB replied: "Yeah, you've trimmed your moustache."

Eligible bachelor?

A Melbourne Cricket Club member took his wife to the cricket for the first time and, as the field settled in for the first ball of the day, a nearby fan commented: "Shane Warne's a good catch."

The member's wife immediately turned around and said: "No he's not; he's married."

...And, for a few last words

A FRUSTRATED WARWICKSHIRE SPECTATOR - To County skipper Brian Lara after the star batsman had failed in a quarter-final of the NatWest Trophy competition in 1998:

"You are getting 200,000 pounds ($A500,000) a year and I have taken a day off work to watch this rubbish."

~~~

BRIAN LARA - In reply:

"I seem to be one of the most hated men here. They are missing the point of being supporters. When times are good you support and equally when times are bad. But that does not seem to be the case at the moment. No player goes out there to lose and if the fans cannot respect that, I can't class them as proper supporters."

~~~

DOUG WALTERS - The great Australian batsman, on streakers:
"When it first occurred it offered us some slight amusement. But after a while it became tiresome and a darn nuisance."

∿∿∿

BILL ALLEY - The veteran Somerset all-rounder in 1967:
"People don't come to see me play any more. They come to see me drop dead from exhaustion or old age."

∿∿∿

MIKE PROCTER - The South African coach on Australian spinners Shane Warne and Tim May in 1994:
"Warne and May are very good bowlers. But they're not world-beaters by any stretch of the imagination. I think they've been fortunate in that they have had very good wickets to bowl on."

∿∿∿

MICHAEL ATHERTON - When appointed England captain in 1993:
"If things start going wrong there'll be criticism, as always. But I think I'm tough enough inwardly to handle that, strong enough to make my own judgments and stand or fall by them."
Atherton had a disastrous run as England captain and stood down less than five years later.

∿∿∿

CHRIS LEWIS - The England all-rounder in an outburst in 1998 after hearing he was not named in the 37-man provisional squad for the World Cup:
"The selectors are full of shit."

∿∿∿

ROGER IDDISON - A member of England's first (1861-2) touring team to Australia:

"I don't think very much of their play but they're a wonderful lot of drinking men."

BHAGWAT CHANDRASEKHAR - The Indian batsman on his reputation for making ducks:

"I certainly don't work at it, yet I seem to be able to get them without too much trouble."

~~~

BHAGWAT CHANDRASEKHAR - On his spin bowling:

"As I'm walking back I think maybe I'll bowl a googly. Then, as I run in, no, I'll bowl a leg-spinner. Then, do you know, just as I prepare to bowl, I decided it'll be a googly after all. And, then, as I let go of the ball, I say, sod it, I'll bowl a top-spinner."

~~~

SIR LEONARD HUTTON - The great England batsman on Australian pace bowler Keith Miller:

"I never felt physically safe against him. He once scared me half to death with unbelievable speed on a docile Adelaide pitch."

~~~

MASANOBU NINOMIYA - A pioneering Japanese cricketer, explaining his favorite aspects of the game:

"We prefer fast bowling in Japan. I like fielding the most because it feels good when I catch a hard ball."

~~~

JACK HOBBS - The great England batsman:
"It always seems to me that cricket would be a better game if the papers didn't publish the averages."

~~~

CHRIS COWDREY - The England batsman on following in the cricketing footsteps of father Colin:
"The name Cowdrey does not mean I can take anything for granted and I'm dismissing suggestions about treading the same path as Dad, who won 114 Test caps."

~~~

CHERYL KERNOT - The then-leader of the Democrats and former cricket umpire in 1994:
"It can get pretty willing on the cricket field but the sledging is probably worse in Parliament because it is continuous and there are more of them."

~~~

LEN HUTTON - The England captain on why he sent Australia in to bat at Brisbane in the 1954-5 series:
"Pitches are like wives; you can never tell how they are going to react."

~~~

MERV HUGHES - The Australian pace bowler on reincarnation:
"Next time around I'm coming back as a big-hitting batter capable of playing all the Calypso shots and more."

~~~

MERV HUGHES' THIRD FORM MATHS TEACHER - In a school report:

"If paying no attention to me and disrupting the rest of the class were important skills in Maths, Merv would be the most skilful mathematician in the school."

~~~

MERV HUGHES' FIFTH FORM GEOGRAPHY TEACHER - In a school report:

"When Merv leaves school, he is going to have to be very good at football and cricket."

~~~

JOHN ARLOTT - The famous English commentator on a "streak" during the England-Australia Test at Lord's in 1975:

"We have got a freaker (read streaker) down the wicket, not very shapely as it is masculine and I would think it has seen the last of its cricket for the day. The police are mustered, so are the cameramen and Greg Chappell. No! He has had his load, he is being embraced by a blond policeman and this may be his last public apperance. But what a splendid one."

~~~

ROBIN SMITH - The England batsman once was quoted as saying:

"Australians have big mouths with bitchy intentions."

~~~

ROBIN SMITH - In denying he made made this comment:
"I am a very sensitive person and wouldn't pass that kind of accusation. The whole thing has been blown out of all proportion and I would never pinpoint anyone about sledging. As far as I am concerned, Australia is no different from the rest of the cricket world on the matter and I haven't had any problems elsewhere."

∿∿∿

BOB WOOLMER - The South Africa coach after the fourth day's play in the deciding Fifth Test against England at Headingley in 1998, with England requiring two wickets and South Africa 37 runs for victory:
"There are 11 overs before they (England) get the new ball and we can chip away at the total. I'm not nervous, My nerves were shot long ago."
England won by 27 runs.

∿∿∿

SIR RICHARD HADLEE - In 1993 on Australian Test captain Allan Border:
"It's a crying shame that Australia no longer offers knighthoods because Allan Border deserves it."

∿∿∿

DAVID FRITH - The editor of *Wisden Cricket Monthly*, on the same theme:
"As for Mr Border, who has moulded and commands what is now perhaps the best team in the world, it's a pity Australia no longer accepts knighthoods."

∿∿∿

PETER MAY - The former England captain, in 1985, on the modern trend for cricket fitness:

"We had different ideas on fitness. To me, my best preparation for batting, bowling and fielding was batting, bowling and fielding. I doubt if many of my contemporaries, especially the older ones, did many exercises. I have often tried to picture (Godfrey) Evans and (Denis) Compton doing press-ups in the outfield before the day's play, but so far have failed miserably."

~~~

SIR DONALD BRADMAN - On grass-roots cricket:

"I have always gone out of my way to emphasise that the health, welfare and future of cricket lies in the hands of the thousands of club and social cricketers who gave birth to the game and nourish its existence."

~~~

NEVILLE CARDUS - The great English cricket writer on the city of churches:

"Adelaide - 100 in the shade and Bradman 300 in the sun."

~~~

TONY CRAFTER - The Australian Test umpire on the difficulties of his craft:

"Whatever you do at the elite level, whether it's sport, work or anything else, it's tough work. Whether you're an umpire, a corporate lawyer or high-flying chief executive of a multi-national company, you have to make decisions that are often unpopular."

~~~

Ian Botham - a holiday suggestion

IAN BOTHAM - The England all-rounder on returning from the 1984 tour of Pakistan:

"Pakistan is the sort of place every man should send his mother-in-law, for a month, all expenses paid."

ARTHUR MAILEY - The Australian leg-spinner of the 1920s on spinners:

"With very few exceptions the great spin bowlers of cricket were personalities and men of character - not always pleasant but invariably interesting. They may have lacked the charm and friendliness of their faster confederates; they may have been more temperamental and less self-disciplined; but there seemed to be an absence of orthodoxy about them and they were able to meander through life as individuals, not as public servants."

~~~

ARTHUR MAILEY - A fulltime butcher and a part-time journalist, the Australian spinner placed this sign across his shop's front window:

"I bowl tripe. I write tripe and I sell tripe."

~~~

HANSIE CRONJE - The South African captain, after losing the Fifth Test (and the series) to England at Headlingley in 1998:

"There are times when you feel umpires give more for the opposition, but you have to accept it."

~~~

ALI BACHER - Managing director of the United Cricket Board of South Africa on controversial decisions by Pakistan umpire Javed Akhtar, who gave nine of the 10 lbw decisions - seven against South Africa - in a 1998 Test at Headingley:

"One prominent England player told me Headingley is an especially difficult wicket to officiate on because of its up-and-down nature. It was wrong to get a chap in from the Indian sub-continent for his first-ever game in England, and a crucial Test match, and put him in at Headingley."

~~~

ALAN DONALD - The South African pace bowler on British radio, discussing the performance of an English umpire in a Test at Trent Bridge in 1998:

"He had a couple of shockers that affected the course of the Test. Like all umpires, he is dealing with people's careers when he is in the middle. He seemed very much under pressure to me, like we all are, and I suppose there comes a time when you decide you have had enough. One decision can swing a game."

CRAIG McDERMOTT - The Australian pace bowler said of West Indies' intimidation:

"The reality is that the West Indians in 1991 did everything (Viv) Richards accused the Australians of doing 16 years earlier. While batting, I sometimes was called a f@#!%^* white coward. That was by no means the worst of the insults. I have no doubt I was singled out for special attention. They picked on me deliberately because they wanted to put me off my game."

PETER BURGE - The burly Queensland and Australian Test batsman on those who criticised him for suggesting he was over-weight:

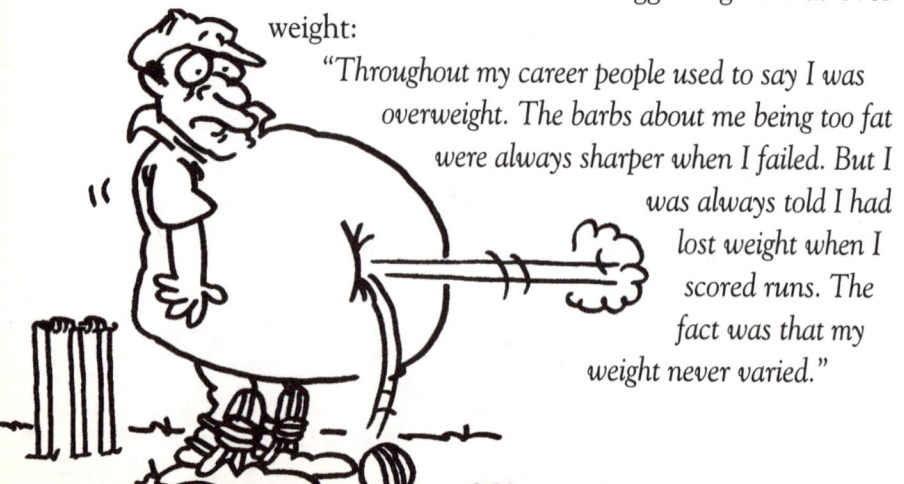

"Throughout my career people used to say I was overweight. The barbs about me being too fat were always sharper when I failed. But I was always told I had lost weight when I scored runs. The fact was that my weight never varied."

SHANE WARNE - The great Australian leg-spinner on his introduction to the craft:

"There was a guy at east Sandringham called Ron Cantlon who used to bowl offies and leggies in our first eleven. I asked him one day: 'How do you do bowl those (leg-spinners)?' He showed me and at first I didn't think much of its but I gave it a try and I enjoyed it. It was just something different from charging in and bowling medium-pace."

~~~

DR W.G. GRACE - On defensive batting:

"I hate defensive strokes. You only get three runs off them."

~~~

DEREK PRINGLE - The England all-rounder on Shane Warne:

"He is cricket's answer to the Great White Shark."

~~~

VIC RICHARDSON - The former Australian Test captain, giving advice to grandson Ian Chappell about the possibility of following in his footsteps by captaining Australia:

"If you ever captain Australia, don't do it like a Victorian."

~~~

IAN CHAPPELL - Appointed captain in 1971, Chappell later interpreted this advice as:

"I was in no doubt that he meant I shouldn't be defensive as a captain. I hope if I ever 'run into him' he shouldn't be too disappointed."

~~~

KERRY PACKER - In 1977 on the introduction of his World
Series Cricket:
*"Cricket is the easiest sport in the world to take over. Nobody bothered
to pay the players what they were worth."*

~~~

KERRY PACKER - On the same theme:
*"If they (the Australian Cricket Board) don't co-operate, they'll walk
straight into a meat mangler."*

~~~

TONY GREIG - The England captain, in 1977, on plans for World
Series Cricket:
*"The plight of the modern cricketer is certainly not the best. Many
who've been playing the game eight years or more are living on the
breadline. In the winter, they go abroad coaching, leaving their families
behind. Test cricketers are also not paid what they're worth. As a result
of this action, cricket may in five or 10 years come into line with tennis
and golf. Then, if a young man is faced with a decision which to play,
he can choose cricket with confidence."*

~~~

IAN CHAPPELL - On South Australian run-machine Jamie
Siddons:
"He's a good, ordinary batsman."

~~~

JAMIE SIDDONS - In reply:
*"Maybe people like Ian Chappell might think I can play a bit when I
start going past him (on Sheffield Shield run lists)."*

~~~

IAN MECKIFF - Many years after being called for "throwing" in the 1963 Brisbane Test against South Africa:

"The last three and a half days of the match I played from memory. I was still a member of the side but I don't remember much about what happened. I basically had to re-think my life over that time."

~~~

RICHIE BENAUD - To Meckiff when removing him from the bowling after being no-balled:

"I'm afraid this is the end."

~~~

FRED TRUEMAN - The great England pace bowler on cricket theorists:

"If there is a game in the world that attracts the half-baked theorists more than cricket, I have yet to hear of it."

~~~

CRAIG McDERMOTT - The Queensland pace bowler, after commentator Tony Greig hinted at ball-tampering in a one-day match against Tasmania in 1993:

"The wicket was crap and the ball was crap. I was just cleaning a bit of crap off it. It's as simple as that. He can say what he likes."

~~~

THE SUNDAY MAIL, BRISBANE - On the Australian selectors' reluctance to name Queenslander Matthew Hayden:

"Cricket prodigy Matthew Hayden is not in the Australian Test team because he is a Queenslander and Queenslanders have to be that much better to achieve recognition."

~~~

TIM MAY - The Australian Test spinner recalling a comment by Victorian coach Les Stillman:

"He said three years ago (1991) there was no place in Sheffield Shield cricket for a spin bowler."

⁓

KEN RUTHERFORD - The New Zealand captain, after a big defeat by Australia in 1993:

"I'm very concerned for our middle order. We've already called on the immediate next people down, so who do you go to next? I've got a four-year-old son who might like a go."

⁓

LEN HUTTON - The England batsman, on the bowling of Australian spinner Bill "Tiger" O'Reilly:

"He nearly bent in two bowling. This business about some bowlers being able to pitch a ball on a dinner plate applied to him and when he appealed he nearly jumped down your throat."

⁓

LEN HUTTON - On Australian batsman David Boon:

"I can visualise him on a sheep farm in Tasmania, sipping lagers on a verandah, the ideal temperament for dealing with fast bowlers."

⁓

DEAN JONES - The Australian batsman on his controversial career:

"Unfortunately, I'm never going to have 100 per cent of the people behind me because of the way I am. I speak from the heart and at times I am too honest. Perhaps I should do things a bit more discreetly or diplomatically, but that's me."

GEOFF BOYCOTT - The former England batsman, as a BBC commentator, on the selection of Ian Salisbury for England against South Africa in 1998:

"He couldn't bowl out my grandmother with a rolling pin."

GRAEME HICK - On a return to international form in a one-day match against Sri Lanka in 1998:

"People have been saying it's my last chance for a few years now, but I don't approach my cricket that way any more."

~~~

ALEC STEWART - The England captain, on Hick's form:

"Graeme had three innings in the Test series (against South Africa) and missed out, but he is a top quality player. If he wasn't, he wouldn't be here (in the England side)."

~~~

RAY LINDWALL - The great Australian fast bowler:

"There's no sitting duck like a scared duck."

~~~

UNKNOWN VICTORIAN REPRESENTATIVE - Batting in the St Kilda club nets, this cricketer told the 15-year-old Keith Miller: *"Throw the ball to someone else, lad. I want some proper practice."* Miller crossed to the South Melbourne club and became one of the greatest all-rounders the game has seen.

≈≈≈

BOB RADFORD - The NSWCA chief executive, stealing a line from then-Prime Minister Paul Keating, on NSW's win in the 1993-4 Sheffield Shield final: *"This is the sweetest win of all."*

≈≈≈

SHANE WARNE - The Australian spinner on sledging: *"I have quickly become an expert on what not to do."*

≈≈≈

MIKE WHITNEY - The former Australian and NSW pace bowler on retirement in 1994: *"I'm going to miss the dressing room. It's a unique place but it's not my turf any more."*

≈≈≈

DAILY EXPRESS - The English newspaper ran this banner headline after England had defeated South Africa 2-1 in the 1998 series in England: *"NOW BRING ON THE AUSSIES!"*

≈≈≈

TONY GREENBERG - The Melbourne-based sports writer wrote this poem in praise of Australia's 1993 Ashes tour:

A is for ASHES, Aussies on fire,
B is for BOONY, the ultimate trier.
C is for CADDICK, only in for his batting,
D is for DELIVERY, the one that got Gatting.
E is for EMBUREY, answering the call,
F is for FOUREX, on every wall.
G is for GOOCH, English captain no more,
H is for HEADLINGLEY, AB the top score.
I is for ILOTT, military medium at best,
J is for JULIAN, he saved the third Test.
K is for KNIGHTHOOD, Sir Mervyn sounds grand,
L is for LORD'S, the great sacred land.
M is for MERV, all heart and mo,
N is for NINEPINS, down the Poms go!
O is for OPENERS, Taylor and Slater so slick,
P is for PITCHES, where spin can do the trick.
Q is for QUEEN, she was there for Test two,
R is for REIFFEL, 'cos he ripped through.
S is for SUMO, a chant from the crowd,
T is for TWINS, Mark and Steve did us proud.
U is for UNIQUE, the English on top,
V is for VIDEO, success or a flop?
W is for WARNE, no praise is too high,
X is for X-RAY, Merv's groin, May's thigh.
Y is for YOUTH, or selectors chose right,
Z is for ZOEHRER, to give Healy a fright!

ALEC STEWART - The England captain, after winning the series against South Africa:

> *"Now we've got to bring home the Ashes. We're ready to face the Aussies together."*

~~~

ALEC STEWART - On defeating South Africa in the deciding Test at Headlingley:

> *"If England wins at anything - the World Cup, a Test match, at tiddlywinks - it makes people happy."*

~~~

MARK WAUGH - The Australian batsman on England's series win over South Africa:

> *"We're not exactly quaking in our boots."*

~~~

MICHAEL ATHERTON - The England batsman and former Test captain on trying to keep the series win in perspective:

> *"I would suggest we keep post-Headingley euphoria to a minimum and cut out reference to the 'Dream Team'."*

~~~

DUNCAN GAWTHORPE - A school headmaster on why England's Darren Gough chose cricket ahead of soccer:

> *"Darren was an outstanding soccer player, brighter than average, but came under the heading 'could have done better'."*

~~~

SHANE WARNE - The Australian spinner on his sledging woes in 1994:

"I had a good talk with Mark Taylor and he was brutally honest with me. He asked me what was happening because it's not the Shane Warne they know. I'm getting frustrated and I haven't been able to relax at all away from the game."

~~~

ALLAN DONALD - The South African pace bowler on playing against Australia:

"You can expect anything playing against Australia. They're a hell of a good outfit and they play Test cricket the hard way. They don't make you feel very welcome out there, which is the way to play Test cricket."

~~~

LEN HUTTON - The England batsman on Australian pace bowler Keith Miller:

"The one player I wanted on my side was Keith Miller. I would have asked him where he wanted to bat and when he wanted to bowl and then left it to him."

~~~

JEFF THOMSON - Talking of the first time he bowled to New Zealand's Martin Crowe, in 1981:

"I knocked his helmet straight off his head. It went to pieces and blood came out...I thought it was brains coming out. I think he was pretty happy to be alive."

~~~

JAVED MIANDAD - The Pakistan batsman on his infamous confrontation with Australian pace bowler Dennis Lillee in 1981:
"I lifted my bat to ward him off and warn him that if he hit me I would hit him back."

~~~

DENNIS LILLEE - In apology for this incident:
"It set a bad example to children and for this, in particular, I am truly sorry."

~~~

ROD MARSH - The former Australian wicketkeeper on confidence in batting:
"I was talking to Boony (David Boon) about bad trots in batting. Fifty people tell you what's wrong and in the end so many people are giving you advice, you're ruined. Instead of one problem, you have 20 because you are trying 50 different solutions. The whole thing is that cricket is a very simple game. The simpler you keep it the better you are."

~~~

ROD MARSH - On knee problems in retirement:
"I kept wickets from the time I was eight years old. You'd have to expect knee problems."

~~~

IMRAN KHAN - The great Pakistani all-rounder on his playboy image:
"When I read articles about 'Imran Khan the sex symbol' I am frankly amazed. Initially, it came as a surprise because I grew up with a complex about being ugly - fostered by my elder sister who remains astonished to this day to read comments about my alleged good looks."

Imran Khan - sex symbol

IMRAN KHAN - On a similar theme:
"The fact that I am shy has been mistaken for arrogance, a charge I've had to live with for almost all my life."

∿∿∿

BILL "TIGER" O'REILLY - The former Australian spinner on the 1989 England team thrashed by Australia:
"They're a team of drongos."

∿∿∿

WEST INDIES FANS - In a chant to pace bowler Uton Dowe after Australian batsman Keith Stackpole had smashed him all over the ground:
"Dowe shall not bowl short."

∿∿∿

STEPHEN BOOK - The New Zealand Test number 11 on his batting:

"I'm not such a bad batsman. It's just that I don't have any luck."

≈≈≈

GREG CHAPPELL - The Australian batsman explaining a return to form for a double century against Pakistan in 1981-2:

"He (six-year-old son Stephen) told me to keep my head down and stop hitting in the air."

≈≈≈

GRAHAM YALLOP - The Australian captain on a difference of opinion with teammate Rodney Hogg in the 1978-9 series against England:

"Hogg suggested we survey the back of the Adelaide Oval, and I don't think he had a tennis match on his mind."

≈≈≈

DENNIS LILLEE - The great Australian pace bowler on retirement in 1984:

"It bugs me that there are two sets of rules. Yes, I've done things that I have regretted. But I think at the time when they are done, they are done in the heat of the moment. But I'm sure I could not have done anything different. It's just me."

≈≈≈

COLIN McCOOL - The Australian batsman on Test teammate Bill O'Reilly:

"Off the field, he could be your life-long buddy, but out in the middle, he had all the loveable qualities of a demented rhinoceros."

≈≈≈

GARY GILMOUR - The NSW all-rounder on the parochialism of fans at the WACA, Perth:

> *"You have to clap yourself on at the WACA."*

〰〰〰

ALLAN BORDER - After captaining Australia in the losing 1985 Ashes series:

> *"It's going to be very hard to convince people back home that we really do have a lot of promising young players."*

〰〰〰

NEVILLE OLIVER - The ABC commentator:

> *"If he (West Indies wicketkeeper Junior Murray) has a child, he'll have to be Junior Murray Senior."*

〰〰〰

A GRAVESTONE - In England:

> *"As in life so in death lies a bat of renown,*
> *Slain by a lorry (three ton);*
> *His innings is over, his bat is laid down;*
> *To the end a poor judge of a run."*

〰〰〰

FRED TRUEMAN - The England fast bowler to a batsman:

> *"You've got more bloody edges than a broken pisspot."*

〰〰〰

CRICKET FAN - Jeering the slow batting of Ken "Slasher" Mackay:

> *"You'll never die of a stroke, Mackay."*

DICKIE BIRD - The popular English umpire:
> *"I've given everything to cricket. I've never married.*
> *I'm married to cricket."*

I DO!

GREG MATTHEWS - The flamboyant Australian spinner on a suggestion that he had a punk haircut:
> *"To call it a punk haircut, I think, was exaggerated. I had a short back and sides, almost a crewie...I always thought my hair was quite conservative."*

ARTHUR MORRIS - The Australian batsman on his "reward" for three Test centuries on the 1946-7 tour of England:
> *"The Australian Board of Control gave me a wristwatch. I wonder what they'd get today?"*

IAN CHAPPELL - On commentating for Channel Nine:
> *"I get nervous. It's like before I was going out to bat."*

GLEN TURNER - The New Zealand batsman on Australia:

"*When you come back from Australia, you feel you've been in Vietnam.*"

~~~

DENNIS LILLEE - After bowling a "bean" ball to England tailender Bob Willis:

"*I know I'm a ruthless bastard, but I wouldn't deliberately put a ball like that on anyone. It slipped.*"

~~~

GEOFF BOYCOTT - The England opener on the West indies:

"*I'd like to paint my face black and go in for the West Indies against our bloody attack.*"

~~~

DENNIS LILLEE - The Australian pace bowler on his craft:

"*Why can't fast bowlers be honest and say: 'I bowl bouncers for one reason and that is to hit the batsman and thus intimidate him.' I try to hit a batsman in the rib cage when I bowl a purposeful bouncer, and I want it to hurt so much that the batsman doesn't want to face me any more.*"

~~~

IAN BOTHAM - The star England all-rounder on England Test captain Mike Brearley:

"I don't know what it is, but I take stuff from him I'd clip other guys in the ear for. There is something about the man. He reads me like a book."

∿∿∿

VIV RICHARDS - The West Indies skipper on Curtly Ambrose after the pace bowler's first tour of Australia, in 1988-9:

"He has the potential to be a world-beater. Come to think of it, he's not far off it now."

∿∿∿

PATSY HENDREN - The England Test cricketer to a fan who had suggested he get a bag after dropping a chance:

"If I had a sack as big as your mouth, I wouldn't have dropped it."

∿∿∿

PAUL SHEAHAN - The former Australian batsman, recalling the famous England victory over Australia in the Fourth Test, at Headlingley, in 1972:

"By a very strange coincidence though, an unknown disease called 'fuserium' attacked the grass on the Headingley wicket. This created a pitch which was perfect for (Derek) Underwood's bowling style. Apparently it is rare, this 'fuserium'. It only attacks an area nine feet wide and 22 yards long. Everywhere else the grass is quite unaffected."

~~~

DEAN JONES - The Australian batsman on being given out lbw by a woman umpire playing with English club Nostell in 1988:

"It was a shocking decision and I found out later that she was the opposition captain's wife."

~~~

NEWSPAPER ADVERTISEMENT - In *The Canberra Times*, after Australian captain Greg Chappell instructed brother Trevor to bowl under-arm to New Zealand in a one-day match at the MCG in 1981:

"The Australian cricket team requires new Test captain. The applicant must be a good all-round sportsman, have a good knowledge of the game and be clean shaven. Applicants are asked to apply in person at the SCG."

~~~

NEVILLE OLIVER - The ABC commentator:

"It (the ball) has been stopped just outside the boundary."

~~~

GEOFF BOYCOTT - The England opening batsman on South African Allan Lamb's selection for England in 1982:

"I don't agree with Allan Lamb playing for England any more than I agreed with Tony Greig and Basil D'Oliveira playing. To play for England you should be born in England and it is too ridiculous for words."

~~~

CRICKET BANNER - Held by a fan during an Australia-England Test at the Adelaide Oval in 1991:

"You'd be pissed too if you'd been here since 9am."

~~~

ROBIN SMITH - The England batsman on his fear that the West Indies might discover a champion sipnner to complement its pace attack:

"I just hope they don't shake a coconut tree in the Caribbean and a black Shane Warne drops out."

~~~

LEN DARLING - The Australian batsman of the '30s on cricket in the '80s.

"I don't like all this jumping around and kissing each other. Every time they take a wicket, it's like they won the FA Cup."

~~~

CRAIG McDERMOTT - The Australian pace bowler on West Indies opening batsman Desmond Haynes:

"He seemed to devote so much of his mental energy to telling us what he thought of us that I am sure it must have been a distraction to him. If he had not talked to us so much, he would have scored even more runs."

OMAR HENRY - The first non-white to play Test cricket for South Africa, Henry said on the eve of his debut, against India in November, 1992:
"Throughout my career I never thought it (South Africa's return to Test cricket) would happen in my time."

~~~

MARK WAUGH - The Australian batsman when asked his most embarrassing moment:
"Playing my first game of cricket and going out to bat with a protector on my knee."

~~~

SHANE WARNE - The Australian leg-spinner on fame:
"You accept it. It's all part of the job and I don't complain, except when you are out to dinner, you are about to take a bite and some bloke shoves a bit of paper in your face and says 'sign this'."

~~~

DEAN JONES - The Australian batsman on a recall in 1994:
"Who would have thought that this would happen three weeks ago when I was sitting on Portsea beach?"

~~~

JIM MAXWELL - The ABC commentator:
"A false shot, but only slightly false."

~~~

CRICKET BANNER - During a lean period for Australia's Greg Chappell against the West Indies:
"Viv (Richards) whacks, Greg quacks."

GEOFF LAWSON - The former Australian pace bowler, a teetotaller, on drinking:
"Cricketers, in particular, are deeply entrenched in the drinking culture. You are expected to spend plenty of time, in the dressing room, or at the bar - drinking some sort of alcohol, usually beer."

〜〜〜

CRICKET FAN - From Sydney's notorious "Hill", to a team trying to remove a stubborn batsman:
"Send for the fire brigade. They'll get him out."

〜〜〜

AN ENGLISH FAN - To England captain Lionel Tennyson at The Oval in 1921, with advice on how to get Australian batsman Herbie Collins to lose concentration after five and a half hours' batting for just 40 runs:
"Why don't you recite him one of your grandfather's poems?"

〜〜〜

IAN BOTHAM - The great England all-rounder on sledging:
"It has become common for players from certain non-English speaking countries to abuse opposing players in their own language. The idea is that they call you anything they like without your realising it, so they get away with it. They would not get away with it with me. Even if a player was speaking Outer Mongolian I would know when I was being sledged."

〜〜〜

JIM LAKER - The English spinner on Australian pace bowler Ray Lindwall:

"He was a great man at a party and played his part in ensuring that no English brewery went out of business through lack of patronage."

〰〰

JAMES BARRIE - The author of *Peter Pan*, in describing Australian pace bowlers Ted McDonald and Dave Gregory during the 1921 tour of England:

"They complement each other superbly, lightning and thunder."

〰〰

CLIVE LLOYD - The West Indies skipper on why his team considered abandoning the 1980 tour of New Zealand:

"We discovered that our best was not good enough in view of a never-ending succession of staggering umpiring decisions which went against us, match after match. It did not matter how we tried, we were thwarted every time by crucial decisions."

〰〰

HAROLD LARWOOD - The England fast bowler, to teammate Les Ames, expressing his fear of a crowd riot during the Bodyline series against Australia:

"If they come over the fence at us, you take the leg-stump for protection. I'll take the middle."

〰〰

AN INSCRIPTION - From England Bodyline series captain Douglas Jardine, on an ashtray he presented to Harold Larwood:

"To Harold for the Ashes 1932-3. From a grateful skipper."

〰〰

MAX WALKER - The Victorian medium-pacer, after bowling Queensland's Greg Chappell in 1981:
"It was great. It's the first time I've hit the timber in 10 years of bowling at Greg."

＊＊＊

MAX WALKER - On Pakistan cricketer Sikander Bakht:
"Ian Callen (Victorian pace bowler) reckons Sikander is so thin he uses his bat cover as a sleeping bag."

＊＊＊

IAN BOTHAM - The great England all-rounder on his reason for hiring a bodyguard in Australia in 1982:
"I sometimes feel I'm back in the Wild West - because some jerk seems to think I'm the fastest gun around."

＊＊＊

BILL TALLON - The Queensland cricker on his State's chances of winning the Sheffield Shield.
"Queensland won't win the Sheffield Shield until they raffle it and Queenslanders buy all the tickets."

＊＊＊

KEITH MILLER - The Australian all-rounder on Don Bradman:
"When he hooked the ball, he could almost choose the picket it was going to hit along the boundary."

＊＊＊

JIM LAKER - The England spinner on Don Bradman:
"As I ran up, Bradman seemed to know what I was going to bowl, where the ball was going to pitch and how many runs he was going to score."

WALLY GROUT - The Australian wicketkeeper, to South African batsman Jackie McGlew, who had just scored 105 runs over a marathon 575 minutes in 1958:
"That must be some sort of record - a long-playing one."

~~~

WISDEN - The cricket bible, in its 1990 edition, ran this comment on Australian bowler Terry Alderman:
"The single reservation is a suspicion that the bowler who played the biggest part in England's overthrow (in the 1989 Ashes series in England), Terry Alderman, received undue co-operation from the umpires in respect of lbw decisions. Of Alderman's 41 wickets, which made him the only bowler twice to take 40 or more wickets in a series, 19 were lbw compared with six bowled."

~~~

PERCY FENDER - The England batsman on a young Don Bradman:
"He's brilliant, but unsound."

~~~

DEREK RANDALL - The England batsman, in 1980, when Australia's Shane Warne was just 11 years of age:
"You do not see many young bowlers developing the art of leg-spin bowling these days...it will be a tragedy if it disappears from the game completely."

~~~

GLEN TURNER - The great New Zealand batsman, in 1970, on his attitude towards being dismissed:
"I regularly wanted to lock myself in the toilet if I got out. I wanted to be alone."

~~~

A SYDNEY BARRACKER - To England batsman Peter Parfitt, who kept padding away balls from Australian leg-spinner Richie Benaud in 1963:
"Why don't yer tie yer bloody bat to yer pad, Parfitt? Then you might make a run."

~~~

ANOTHER SYDNEY BARRACKER - To New South Welshman Jim Burke for scoring slowly:
"I wish you were a statue and I were a pigeon."

~~~

BILL O'REILLY - The great Australian spinner's advice to a young hopeful:
"Have nothing to do with coaches. In fact, if you should see one coming, go and hide behind the pavilion until he goes away."

~~~

BISHAN BEDI - The Indian spinner on the standard of umpiring in a Test in Australia in 1977:
"We don't swear on the field, but how can you hide your emotions? We Indians are human beings."

~~~

TONY GREIG - The England star on why Geoff Boycott turned down an offer to play World Series Cricket:

"His ability to be where the fast bowlers aren't has long been a talking point among cricketers."

~~~

BARRY RICHARDS - The great South African batsman on cricket bible, *Wisden*:

"Wisden is about as appealling to me as a telephone directory."

~~~

DEAN JONES - The Australian batsman on facing the West Indies:

"If you're prepared to cop a couple of balls in the stomach and maybe one in the head or on the fingers, you might be all right."

~~~

IMRAN KHAN - The Pakistani cricket legend, in his book *All Round View*, on cricket in his country:

"The history of Pakistani cricket is one of nepotism, inefficiency, corruption and constant bickering. It is also the story of players who have risen above the mire. A cricketer needs immense talent, belief in himself and sheer luck to survive the political maze of our cricket."

~~~

BOB WILLIS - The former England captain and fast bowler on the appointment of Mike Atherton as England captain:

"At last we have an intelligent man in charge."

~~~

TERRY ALDERMAN - The Australian swing bowler on being tackled and struck by an England fan during a Test at the WACA in 1982:

"I have played a bit of Aussie Rules football and I know what a gentle tap is, and what a thump to the head is. It was a thump to the head."

▼▼▼

DENNIS LILLEE - The great Australian fast bowler on Australian Test skipper Allan Border:

"If he was an American they would build a monument in his honor."

▼▼▼

GEOFF LAWSON - The Australian fast bowler, on touring Pakistan:

"I usually eat four or five times a day, but I just didn't want to risk it often. You'd never know when you'd go down with three-day stomach cramps and wake up shaking and in a fever. And you couldn't drink the water. I was drinking 20 bottles of Coke a day."

▼▼▼

GEOFF BOYCOTT - As a television commentator, when the England team left for Australia for the 1979-80 tour:

"Everybody that bats is going to have to hang on in there, baby!"

▼▼▼

ROSS EDWARDS - The Australian batsman on the pressure of cricket at the highest level:

"Test cricket has never been a game."

▼▼▼

BILL LAWRY - The pigeon-fancying captain of Australia, comparing his two great sporting loves:

"It's much harder to win a big pigeon race than it is to make a Test hundred."

~~~

MERV HUGHES - The Australian pace bowler on allegations that his teammates had used racial taunts during a Test match against Sri Lanka at Hobart in 1990.

"I thought I had been playing in a different game when I picked up the newspapers to see the headlines. There was nothing I heard out there over the Bellerive Oval that isn't said in any close contest and I've played cricket at all levels."

~~~

JEFF THOMSON - The Australian fast bowler on his technique:
"I just shuffle in and go whang."

IMRAN KHAN - The Pakistan captain advocating the use of neutral umpires:
"People have to accept that there's no doubt that home umpiring now is a big factor."

≈

DAVID LLOYD - The England coach after questioning the bowling action of Sri Lankan spinner Muttiah Muralitharan in 1998:
"I am sorry for the offence that I have caused. I am glad the whole affair is over."

≈

MUTTIAH MURALITHARAN - The Sri Lankan spinner on whether Lloyd should have been sacked:
"It's not my problem. I don't care what happens to him."

≈

ARJUNA RANATUNGA - The Sri Lanka captain on the same issue:
"If the idea was to undermine Muttiah it backfired. It gave strength to him and made him even more determined. No coach should make comments like that."

≈

DAVID LLOYD - The England coach after England had drawn a Test with Zimbabwe in 1996-7:
"We murdered them and they know it. We flippin' hammered them."

≈

ALISTAIR CAMPBELL - The Zimbabwe captain, on Lloyd's comment:
""They're clutching at thin air as far as I'm concerned, and conning themselves into thinking they've played well."

<hr />

H.L. "STORK" HENDRY - The former Australian Test batsman on cricket fans of his era, the '20s:
"They knew their cricket, unlike the galahs that go to (Kerry) Packer one-day games."

<hr />

RICHIE BENAUD - The Channel Nine commentator and former Australian Test captain on the Pakistan bribery scandal:
"There was a bookmaker in England (William Hill) who had an adage that you never bet on anything that talks."

<hr />

RICHIE BENAUD - On how he would react if someone had offered him a bribe during his cricket career:
"I'd have thought the guy had gone off his head, or was about to."

<hr />

MARK TAYLOR - The Australian captain, on the Pakistani scandal:
"We have to make sure we're not too quick to judge people."

<hr />

MARK WAUGH - The Australian batsman on the prospect of facing 35-year-old Antigua veteran Curtley Ambrose at the 1998 Kuala Lumpur Commonwealth Games:

"He's a bit smarter these days. He cranks it up when he has to. He just gets in a good rhythm and he's hard to score off. He's still capable of bowling as quick as anyone."

~~~

STEVE WAUGH - The Australian batsman also on Ambrose and the Commonwealth Games:

"It will be interesting if we have to bat first thing in the morning. He'll be interesting at three or four in the afternoon, too."

~~~

KIM HUGHES - The Australian Test captain on great English all-rounder Ian Botham:

"Don't try to change him or the way he plays. Do that and you've lost your chance of winning Test matches."

~~~

MARK TAYLOR - The Australian captain, on why Sheffield Shield programs should not be reduced in favor of more one-day games:

"We'd lose the basics, which are foot next to ball, hit the ball, run."

~~~

GREG MATTHEWS - The NSW and Australia all-rounder on his image:

"Punk? I've never been a punk in my life. I'm a capitalist, man. Punks are anit-capitalist. People say I have a punk haircut, but there's nothing much I can do with my hair because there isn't much left."

~~~

PETER BURGE - The Australian and Queensland batsman after being offered a cup of tea following a long innings for his State:
"No, I'm stuffed; I feel more like a double rum."

∿∿∿

MIKE GATTING - The former England captain on the selection of Surrey's Ben Hollioake to tour Australia in 1988-9 ahead of several more fancied all-rounders:
"People have suggested that there is a Surrey bias and it's a pretty fair question."

∿∿∿

STEVE WAUGH - The Australian batsman on India's Amay Kgurasiya being forced from the ground through dehydration while fielding during a Commonwealth Games match at Kuala Lumpur in 1998:
"When you see an Indian player collapse with sunstroke or whatever, you know it's hot."

∿∿∿

IAN CHAPPELL - The Channel Nine commentator and former Australian Test captain on Mike Kasprowicz during the Kuala Lumpur Commonwealth Games:
"He's almost too nice a bloke to be a fast bowler."

∿∿∿

ATO BOLDON - The Trinidad track and field sprint star, after watching cricket at the Kuala Lumpur Commonwealth Games:
"I think if I weren't running I'd take up cricket. It seems to me that you don't have to expend much energy playing cricket compared with other sports."

ERNIE JONES - The Australian fast bowler, on the great Dr W.G. Grace:
"The first ball I sent whizzin' through his whiskers; after that he kept hitting me off his blinkin' ear-'ole for four."

∼∼∼

SHAKOOR RANA - The Pakistani umpire, on his infamous run-in with England captain Mike Gatting at Faisalabad in 1987:
"I am reporting Gatting to the Test and County Cricket Board, the tour manager Peter Lush and the Pakistan Board for using foul and abusive language. No captain has spoken to me like that before."

∼∼∼

MIKE GATTING - The England captain complaining about the standard of umpiring in Pakistan after the previous Test, at Lahore:
"It's nice to be able to compete on an even basis, but obviously during this match we weren't competing on an even basis. When we come to Pakistan the umpiring always seems to be the same. But I've never seen it as blatant as this."

∼∼∼

MIKE GATTING - On the same theme:
"All I can ask is that we go out and compete. But if the umpiring is the same as here, it doesn't matter what we do. We can't win."

∼∼∼

BOB COWPER - The Australian batsman to teammates after scoring 307 over 12 hours and 11 minutes against England at the MCG in 1966:
"My God, that must have been the most boring innings you've ever had to sit through."

BOB SIMPSON - The Australian coach on the standard of umpiring during the 1988 tour of Pakistan following a defeat in the First Test at Karachi:

"We did not get one leg-before decision, but Pakistan got six. It seems strange."

～～～

ALLAN BORDER - The Australian captain on the same theme:

"I don't believe it is worth coming here unless there is a change. The wicket was ridiculous and the decisions given against us were atrocious."

～～～

INTIKHAB ALAM - On Australia's complaints:

"We won fairly and squarely. We outclassed the Australians."

～～～

STAN McCABE - The Australian batsman to his father just before he went out to bat during one of the Tests in the 1932-3 Bodyline series:

"If I happen to get hit out there, keep Mum from jumping the fence."

〰

JEFF THOMSON - The Australian fast bowler on missing selection for the 1981 tour of England:

"I've always thought the selectors were a bunch of idiots. All they've done now is confirm it."

〰

KEN MACKAY - The notoriously slow Australian and Queensland batsman before his last appearance for his State at the MCG, in 1963:

"This'll be the last time I play here, so tell the crowd they only have four days to get stuck into me."

〰

BILL LAWRY - The Channel Nine commentator, as Trevor Chappell was about to bowl underarm against New Zealand at the MCG:

"It looks to me like they're going to bowl an underarm off the last ball - this is possibly a little disappointing."

〰

ROBERT MULDOON - The New Zealand Prime Minister on this incident:

"It was the most disgusting effort I can recall in the history of cricket, a game which used to be played by gentlemen."

〰

MALCOLM FRASER - The Australian Prime Minister on this incident:

"At a minimum, Greg Chappell (the Australian captain) should apologise."

~~~

BRAD YOUNG - The Australian spinner on his Commonwealth Games hat-trick against New Zealand at Kuala Lumpur in 1998:

"I now hope I don't have to go back to full-time work for a while."

~~~

BRAD YOUNG - On the first of his hat-trick wicket (Matt Bell, caught Ricky Ponting):

"I dropped it a bit short and Ricky took a good catch behind point."

~~~

BRAD YOUNG - On the second wicket (Daniel Vettori, caught Tom Moody):

"It got the outside edge and clipped the glove of the wicketkeeper (Adam Gilchrist)."

~~~

BRAD YOUNG - On the third wicket (Paul Wiseman, caught Tom Moody):

"I wasn't really thinking I could get a hat-trick. I just thought 'put it around the mark and if something happens like a bat-pad, it happens.' It turned and Tom's big hands worked...easy."

~~~

STEVE WAUGH - The Australian captain on Young's hat-trick:
"Everyone was excited out there. Possibly this is the last time cricket will be in the Commonwealth Games, so whatever you do is history. He (Young) will never forget it."

~~~

STEVE WAUGH - On the Commonwealth Games:
"It's been one of the best weeks of my life. We have seen as much as we could - hockey, weightlifting, gymnastics, swimming, the synchronised swimming and the athletics."

~~~

STEVE WAUGH - On Australia being defeated by South Africa in the final of the Commonwealth Games tournament:
"All the work accounts for nothing now. The players will have to look at themselves and see what they need to do so we play better next time we make a final. We were just outplayed on the day."

~~~

STEVE WAUGH - On his own form at the Commonwealth Games (he scored a not-out century and followed up with 90 not out in the final against South Africa):
"It counts for nothing; I'd swap it all for a gold medal."

~~~

STEVE WAUGH - On future Commonwealth Games prospects:
"I might not be there, but the Australians would like another chance to win it in Manchester (2002), but we just don't know what is going on there (whether cricket will be played at these Games)."

~~~

Joe Darling - good judge

JOE DARLING - The Australian Test captain to England counterpart Archie MacLaren before the final day's play in a 1902 Test, with England requiring just 87 runs with all wickets standing:
"We've only got to shift a few of you and the rest will shiver with fright."
Australia won by three runs.

〜〜〜

C.B. FRY - The great English cricketer on Australia's Hugh Trumble, in 1904:
"It is his head - that long, solemn head - I should fear in England this summer...not his bowling arm, spinning finger, deft as they are. It is the head, best in the side, that makes all the difference for the Australians."

〜〜〜

BILL O'REILLY - The great Australian spinner on why he was not looking forward to touring England in 1938:

"You can take it from me that cricket quickly ceases to be fun once you have settled into the round eternal of six days cricket per week through a four-and-a-half-month tour. As you rise from your couch each morning, you eventually find yourself saying, 'Oh God, not another day's cricket'."

~~~

ARTHUR MORRIS - The Australian batsman on England's Trevor "Barnacle" Bailey:

"If there were 22 Trevor Baileys playing in a match, who would ever go and watch it?

~~~

MIKE GATTING - The former England captain on his achievements in cricket, after retiring from the first-class scene in 1998:

"There was playing for England and being captain when we last won the Ashes. The OBE was special, too, even if other people said it was for Other Buggers' Efforts."

~~~

MIKE GATTING - Still on his cricket achievements:

"All the trophies and statistics in Wisden are nice, but the most important thing is really enjoying the game. That's what I've done."

~~~

MIKE GATTING - After declining to eat a roast lunch during his final match, for Middlesex against Derbyshire:

"It's not easy to run up and down on a full stomach."

~~~

FRED TRUEMAN - The former England fast bowler on newcomer Ben Hollioake during the 1997 Ashes series:

"He made an appearance at a dinner at which I was speaking and was given the sort of reception that used to be reserved for the Beatles and is now kept for the Spice Girls."

~~~

SHANE WARNE - On his progress since bowling England's Mike Gatting with his first ball in a Test on English soil, in 1993:

"The difference between the ball I bowled to Mike Gatting in 1993 and now? About 10,000 overs and four years of wear and tear."

~~~

MATTHEW ELLIOTT - The Australian batsman after scoring a century at Lord's in 1997:
> *"With all the rain breaks, I felt as though I'd opened the batting 20 times."*

⌇⌇⌇

JIMMY MAHER - The Queensland batsman, after his State had won the Sheffield Shield in 1996-7, grabbed a flight steward's microphone on the way back to Brisbane from Perth and said:
> *"Ladies and gentlemen, fasten your seatbelts, place your trays in the upright position. Queensland has won the Sheffield Shield."*

⌇⌇⌇

DESMOND HAYNES - The West Indies opening batsman on making a duck in his last first-class innings:
> *"I spoke to Don Bradman and I said: 'If it's good enough for you, it's good enough for me'."*

⌇⌇⌇

NEWSPAPER HEADLINE - *The London Sun* ran this headline after Australia's Merv Hughes gave abusive fans the middle-finger sign:
> *"UP YOURS - Merv's one-finger salute as fans call him a fat b****d".*

⌇⌇⌇

ALEC STEWART - The England batsman and 'keeper before the 1997 Ashes series in England:
> *"I've been in a few Ashes series now and never been on the winning side. It's about time we put the record straight."*
> *Australia retained the Ashes.*

⌇⌇⌇

NEWSPAPER ADVERTISEMENT - An English newspaper, launching a quest for potential Test fast bowlers:

"You don't have to be a cricketer, just big and strong and reckon you can bowl."

⌁⌁⌁

DAVE RICHARDSON - The South African Test wicketkeeper on a sledging duel between teammate Paul Adams and Australia's Glenn McGrath:

"He (Adams) knows what 'wanker' means. He's learnt it, but I don't know that Glenn McGrath knows what was being said to him in Afrikaans."

⌁⌁⌁

MICHAEL BEVAN - The Australian batsman on twice being stranded in the '80s in Test innings:

"Once he (Glenn McGrath) walks out to bat and you are in the 80s, you know you've got to get a move on."

⌁⌁⌁

TONY GREIG - The Channel Nine commentator on a poor fielding effort by the West Indies' Curtly Ambrose:

"He's had a Barry Crocker (shocker)."

⌁⌁⌁

BANNER - In reference to a string of failures by West Indies batsman Brian Lara:

"Mother Teresa, Brian Lara...who'll make the next century?"

⌁⌁⌁

ALLAN BORDER - The Australian Test captain on sledging:
"It's not tiddlywinks out there. It's Test cricket."

~~~

ALLAN BORDER - On the same theme:
"Chirping is part of the game. If you can't handle it, you've got to get out of it (cricket), really."

~~~

MATTHEW ELLIOTT - The Australian and Victorian opening batsman on the mid-wicket collision with Mark Waugh, just before the Melbourne Boxing Day Test against the West Indies in 1997 (Elliott injured a knee):
"You visit Queensland and everyone's yelling out, 'Where's Hayden?'. I get to NSW and it's 'Where's Slater?'. I was hoping to get to Melbourne so people wouldn't be canning me all the time."

~~~

MATTHEW ELLIOTT - On his collision with Mark Waugh:
"I need some blinkers, like the horses, so I can run in a straight line... I think Mark needs them as well."

~~~

ADAM PARORE - The New Zealander, to Darryl Cullinan - regarded as Shane Warne's "bunny" - after Chris Harris had bowled to the South African:
"Bowled Warnie!"

~~~

SHANE WARNE - The Australian leg-spinner on India's Sachin Tendulkar:
"I think I'll got to bed tonight and have nightmares about him hitting me over my head for six."

~~~

MARK TAYLOR - The Australian Test captain on Mark Waugh's 153 not out when ill in a Test against India in 1998:
"I'm going to give him some (Indian) water and make him crook before every game."

~~~

CHRISTIAN VIERI - The Italian World Cup soccer star, who played cricket as a boy in Australia, on idol Allan Border:
"They told me he's going to send me a bat and I'm really happy about that. I'll be sending him one of my jerseys in return."

~~~

DENNIS LILLEE - The former Australian pace star on former teammate Greg Chappell's new health diet:
"It'd kill me if I went on to something healthy."

~~~

SHAKOOR RANA - The former Pakistani umpire on the English media:
"They find a ghost in everything - the air, the food, the hotels - and also mock our culture. I will not even wrap a fish in these tabloids."

~~~

STEVE WAUGH - The Australian Test batsman, after winning two cars and $140,000 for hitting an advertising sign during the summer of 1995-6:
> *"Everything is split up, but I get the tax problem."*

∿∿∿

DAVID BOON - At his farewell party after Australian Test captain Mark Taylor kissed him on the cheek:
> *"I'm just glad it wasn't quite as wet as a Merv Hughes kiss."*

∿∿∿

SHANE WARNE - The Australian leg-spinner on fast bowlers:
> *"They're bloody meatheads. We're the blokes who gamble. We're the least screwed up. The quicks are mad blokes."*

∿∿∿

MIKE HAYSMAN - Commentating on a caught and bowled by New Zealand's Mark Greatbatch:
> *"One of the hardest things is to take a caught and bowled off your own bowling."*

∿∿∿

DENNIS LILLEE - On England opening batsman Geoff Boycott (in jest):
> *"Geoffrey is the only fellow I've met who fell in love with himself at a young age and has remained faithful ever since."*

∿∿∿

STUART LAW - After failing to score for Australia A and then being promoted to the Australian one-day side:
> *"I obviously impressed. It was a good duck."*

ADAM GILCHRIST - The WA and Australian batsman-wicketkeeper after a spell by South Africa's Allan Donald:
"That was the fastest bowling I've seen; or rather, didn't see."

⌇⌇⌇

COLIN INGLEBY-MACKENZIE - The Marylebone Cricket Club, after a vote in 1998 to admit women to the 211-year-old club:
"It's a great thing for the game. There will be a better atmosphere in the club."

⌇⌇⌇

COLIN INGLEBY-MACKENZIE - On a suggestion that the MCC might create an all-male bar:
"I'm a member of Sunningdale Golf Club and the Turf Club. They have all-male bars as well as mixed and the atmosphere there allows gentlemen to discuss gentlemen's matters."

⌇⌇⌇

AN MCC MEMBER - Obviously disgruntled after the announcement of the vote, this unnamed member was quoted as saying:
"They might as well bulldoze Lord's. I'll never go there again."

⌇⌇⌇

RACHEL HEYHOE-FLINT - The former England captain, on the MCC vote:
"It's been well worth waiting for, but I still have to wait and see if I am going to be admitted."

⌇⌇⌇

DICKIE BIRD - The English umpire, on his relationship with
Pakistan Test teams:
*"I'd try to have a laugh and a joke with the Pakistanis, try to calm them
down because they can get a bit over-excited. I couldn't understand a
word they were saying most of the time, but then I don't suppose too
many of them understood my Yorkshire accent."*

WASIM AKRAM - The former Pakistan Test captain, in 1998 on
the bribery row:
*"I've never been offered any money to fix a match. Never, ever. I am
innocent and always have been. I always give my best and I wouldn't
do such a stupid thing with little pennies."*

WASIM AKRAM - On being named in the row:
*"How can the judge who wrote the interim report implicate anything on
me without cross-examining me? It was a one-sided story backed up by
people who don't like me in the board itself. It's people who want their
sons, their relatives to play in the side. "*

THE DAWN - The Pakistan newspaper, on this row:
*"(Salim) Malak said that getting himself run out was nothing new for
Inzamam, who 60 per cent of the time was out this way."*

ABDUL QADIR - In Australia in 1998 to play with Melbourne District club Carlton, the former Pakistan Test leg-spinner, had this to say on the bribery row:
"I am straightforward and honest and (if I say anything) I will go back to Pakistan and will be straight in the courts."

∼∼∼

ABDUL QADIR - On leg-spin bowling:
"I have an art and I should deliver my art to the artists."

∼∼∼

MARK BOSNICH - Australian and Aston Villa (English Premier League) soccer goalkeeper on cricket:
"Ever since I was a kid, I've dreamed of playing on the MCG. Strangely enough, my dreams have never involved playing soccer. Instead, I have always imagined myself dressed in whites, face covered in zinc and cricket ball in hand."

∼∼∼

ALI BACHER - The South African cricket boss, on Protea captain Hansie Cronje being banned from commenting on the umpiring in the 1998 Test series in England:
"The captain's tongue is handcuffed."

∼∼∼

DEAN JONES - The Victorian batsman, after being told in 1997 that a 406-minute century, against Queensland, was the slowest ever at the MCG:
"Surely Bill (Lawry) would have been a bit slower."

∼∼∼

ALLAN BORDER - One the Canberra Comets' recruitment of Merv Hughes:
> *"He's the sightscreen, isn't he?"*

〜〜

MAGAZINE ADVERTISEMENT - An Indian magazine, promoting Australia's Waugh twins:
> *"If one twin gets a stomach upset, the other gets the runs."*

〜〜

IAN HEALY - The Australian Test 'keeper on injuries:
> *"A broken finger is no excuse to miss a Test."*

〜〜

IAN HEALY - On wicketkeeping:
> *"You rarely see 'keepers playing in social or benefit games when they retire. They are normally buggered. It's a job that takes a lot out of you. Once you've had it, that's that."*

〜〜

SHANE WARNE - One his balcony celebrations after the Australian Test win over England at Trent Bridge in 1997:
> *"I didn't drop my pants and moon the crowd; I just went a little bit over the top. I carried on like a pork chop, but the bottom line was I didn't do anything wrong."*

〜〜

IAN HEALY - On his world-record 356th Test victim, at Rawalpindi, Pakistan, in October, 1998:
> *"It was like being on a duck or 99 for 150 overs."*

〜〜

Ian Healy - no excuses

IAN HEALY - On the same theme:
"I moved very naturally today and I didn't really care. Half the blokes forgot about it because we had a sniff of victory and then it clicked 'shit, that's it!' when it happened."

〰〰〰

ROD MARSH - The former Australian 'keeper, on sending Healy a bottle of champage to celebrate breaking his record:
"It's a dry old place over there (Pakistan) so I hope he enjoys it."

Mark Taylor's run-spree

Believe it or not, there was a ridiculous inference in Pakistan after Mark Taylor's 334 not out in the second Test at Peshawar in October, 1998, that the Australian captain had helped bookmakers in NOT passing the world record of 375 by the West Indies' Brian Lara at St John's, Antigua, in 1993-4.

Australian team manager Steve Bernard replied, he (the writer) "should be working for Walt Disney".

After being bowled by Aamir Sohail, Taylor said: "I was hoping to get another hundred then see what happened. I'm a little disappointed, I suppose, but I'd be pretty happy to make 420 runs in every Test match".

Taylor's secret? According to his wife Judi, the Australian captain breakfasted on "horse's meal" during a fitness campaign devised by his Sydney trainer Kevin Chevell. The "horse's meal" comprised raw oats, honey, fruit and steamed vegetables.

Bibliography

Books and other publications used in research:

Arlott, John - *The Ashes* (Pelham Books)

Barrett, Norman - *The Daily Telegraph Chronicle of Cricket* (The Daily Telegraph)

Blainey, Geoffrey - *A Game of Our Own* (Information Australia)

Bromby, Robin - *A Century of Ashes* (Resolution Press)

Coleman, Robert - *Seasons in the Sun* (Hargreen)

Crook, Frank - *Talking Cricket* (ABC Books)

Daniel, Mark - *World Famous Sporting Events* (Parragon)

Davidson, Alan - *Fifteen Paces* (Souvenir Press)

Dawson, Graham and Wat, Charlie - *Test Cricket Lists* (Five Mile Press)

Egan, Jack - *Extra Cover* (Pan Books)

Frith, David - *The Fast Men* (Richard Smart Publishing)

Golesworthy, Maurice - *The Encyclopedia of Cricket* (The Sportsmans Book Club)

Harte, Chris - *A History of Australian Cricket* (Andre Deutsch)

Martin-Jenkins, Christopher and Gibson, Pat - *Summers Will Never Be The Same* (Partridge Press)

Murphy, Patrick - *Botham: A Biography* (J.M. Dent and Sons)

Pollard, Jack - *From Bradman to Border - Australian Cricket 1948-89* (Angus and Robertson)

Robertson-Glasgow, R.C. - *Rain Stopped Play* (Dennis Dobson Ltd.)

Ross, Gordon - *The Gillette Book of Cricket and Football* (Gillette Razor Co.)

Salberg, Derek - *Much Ado About Cricket* (K.A.F. Brewin Books)

Smith, Rick - *ABC Guide to Australian Test Cricketers* (ABC Books)

Synge, Allen and Cooper, Leo - *Tales From Far Pavilions* (Arrow)

Walters, Doug - *One for the Road* (Swan)

Whitington, R.S. - *An Illustrated History of Australian Cricket* (Currey O'Neil)

Whitington, R.S. - *The Quiet Australian - The Lindsay Hassett Story* (Heinemann)

Numerous newspapers and cricket magazines, including *Cricketer* and *Inside Edge*